U.S. Fish & Wildlife Service

Status Review and Conservation Recommendations for the Gull-billed Tern (*Gelochelidon nilotica*) in North America

Biological Technical Publication

BTP-R1013-2010

Larry Ditto©

U.S. Fish & Wildlife Service

Status Review and Conservation Recommendations for the Gull-billed Tern (*Gelochelidon nilotica*) in North America

Biological Technical Publication
BTP-R1013-2010

Kathy C. Molina[1]

R. Michael Erwin[2]

Eduardo Palacios[3]

Eric Mellink[4]

Nanette W. H. Seto[5,6]

[1] Natural History Museum of Los Angeles County, Los Angeles, CA

[2] U.S. Geological Survey, Patuxent Wildlife Research Center, University of Virginia, Charlottesville, VA

[3] Centro de Investigación Científica y de Educación Superior de Ensenada (CICESE Unidad La Paz), Pronatura Noroeste, A.C., La Paz, B.C.S. México

[4] Centro de Investigación Científica y de Educación Superior de Ensenada (CICESE), Ensenada, B.C., México

[5] U.S. Fish and Wildlife Service, Migratory Birds and Habitat Programs, Portland, OR

[6] Current Address: Migratory Bird Management, Arlington, VA

Cover image: Gull-billed Tern
Photo credit: Larry Ditto©

Author contact information:

Kathy C. Molina
Natural History Museum of Los Angeles County
Section of Ornithology
900 Exposition Blvd.
Los Angeles, CA 90007
Phone: (213) 763-3368
E-mail: kmolina@nhm.org

R. Michael Erwin
U.S. Geological Survey
Patuxent Wildlife Research Center
Department of Environmental Sciences
University of Virginia
291 McCormick Rd.
Charlottesville, VA 22904
Phone: (434) 924-3207
E-mail: rme5g@virginia.edu

Eduardo Palacios
Centro de Investigación Científica y de Educación
Superior de Ensenada
(CICESE Unidad La Paz)
Pronatura Noroeste
A.C., Miraflores 334 e/ Mulegé y La Paz. Fracc.
Bella Vista
La Paz, B.C.S. 23050
México
Phone: (612) 121-3031, Ext. 111
E-mail: epalacio@cicese.mx

Eric Mellink
Centro de Investigación Científica y de Educación
Superior de Ensenada
(CICESE)
Km 107 Carr. Tijuana-Ensenada
Ensenada, B.C.
México
U.S. Mailing Address:
P. O. Box 434844
San Diego, CA 92143-4844
Phone: (646) 175-0500
E-mail: emellink@cicese.mx

Nanette W. H. Seto (Current Address):
U.S. Fish and Wildlife Service
Migratory Bird Management
4401 N Fairfax Drive, MBSP 4107
Arlington, VA 22203
Phone: (703) 358-1835
E-mail: nanette_seto@fws.gov

For additional copies or information, contact:

U.S. Fish and Wildlife Service
Pacific Southwest Region, Migratory Birds Program
2800 Cottage Way
Sacramento, CA 95825

Recommended citation:

Molina, K. C., R. M. Erwin, E. Palacios, E. Mellink, and N. W. H. Seto. 2010. Status review and conservation recommendations for the Gull-billed Tern (*Gelochelidon nilotica*) in North America. U.S. Department of Interior, Fish and Wildlife Service, Biological Technical Publication, FWS/BTP-R1013-2010, Washington, D.C.

Series Senior Technical Editor:

Stephanie L. Jones
U.S. Fish and Wildlife Service, Region 6
Nongame Migratory Bird Coordinator
P.O. Box 25486
Denver Federal Center
Denver, Colorado 80225-0486

Table of Contents

List of Figures

List of Tables

Executive Summary

The Gull-billed Tern (*Gelochelidon nilotica*) is a medium-sized tern that breeds in small, scattered, often ephemeral colonies, typically in habitat devoid of vegetation near marine waters or saline lakes. In North America, the species breeds along the Atlantic coast south of New York, the Gulf of Mexico, and the Pacific coast of California and Mexico. Its distribution has contracted from known historic range along the Atlantic Coast, but has expanded along the Pacific Coast. Range changes in Mexico are unknown due to fragmentary knowledge of historical colony locations, but some range contraction may have occurred. Two subspecies (*G. n. aranea* and *G. n. vanrossemi*) occur in North America. The current population of *G. n. aranea* in the United States is estimated to be approximately 3610 pairs, over 60% of which occur in Texas. The number of birds in Texas appears stable, but the number of individuals has declined in Maryland, Delaware, Virginia, North Carolina, Florida, and possibly Georgia. *G. n. vanrossemi* has 737 to 808 pairs breeding in western Mexico and southern California.

Gull-billed Terns are designated as a Bird of Conservation Concern by the U.S. Fish and Wildlife Service. *G. n. aranea* is designated as endangered, threatened or of management concern in nine states and *G. n. vanrossemi* is designated as a Bird Species of Special Concern in California.

The main causes of population declines in North America are disturbance of nesting colonies, loss of natural nesting islands, and development or modification of upland foraging habitats. This species often nests on artificially deposited substrates, suggesting it could respond to management of breeding habitat.

Management priorities for Gull-billed Terns are: (1) protection of known nesting colony sites; (2) enhancement and conservation of potential nesting and foraging areas; (3) predator control; (4) development of population viability models; and (5) resolution of conflicts with other species and aquaculture. Research and monitoring needs are: (1) resolution of the subspecific identity of birds breeding in North America; (2) demographic studies addressing population viability; (3) the identification and linkage of breeding and non-breeding ranges; (4) studies of habitat use and ecology during the breeding and non-breeding seasons, especially in Mexico and Central America; (5) continued monitoring of breeding colonies, particularly in the Gulf Coast of Mexico; and (6) the establishment of monitoring efforts in the West Indies.

Acknowledgments

We thank the following colonial waterbird survey coordinators, database managers, breeding bird atlas managers and researchers for graciously providing unpublished information: David H. Allen (North Carolina), David F. Brinker (Maryland), J. Steve Calver (Georgia), Susan E. Cameron (North Carolina), Roger B. Clay (Alabama), Brian E. Collins (California), Michelle L. Gibbons (New York), Philip Glass (Texas), Joe A. Halbrook (Texas), Howard Horne (Alabama), C. David Jenkins (New Jersey), Paul L. Leberg and Gary D. Lester (Louisiana), Tim Manolis (California), Robert W. McFarlane (Texas), Thomas C. Michot (Louisiana), Thomas M. Murphy (South Carolina), James F. Parnell (North Carolina), Robert T. Patton (California), Elisa Peresbarbosa (Mexico), Robert D. Purrington (Louisiana), James A. Rodgers (Florida), Martha Roman (Mexico), Henry "Hank" T. Smith (Florida), Todd Stefanic (California), Mary P. Stevens (Mississippi), Jenny Thompson (Mississippi), Barry R. Truitt (Virginia), Vincent V. Turner (New Jersey), Xicotencatl Vega Picos (Mexico), Michael R. Wasilco (New York), Bryan D. Watts and Bill Williams (Virginia), Jennifer K. Wilson (Texas), and Brad Winn (Georgia). We are grateful to Steven W. Cardiff, Mark A. Goodman, William H. Howe, Gregory D. Jackson, Robert W. McFarlane, David J. Newstead, Robert D. Purrington, Mary P. Stevens, Dorie S. Stolley and Jennifer K. Wilson for responding to numerous requests and providing additional information. We are particularly grateful for the help provided by Roger B. Clay, Philip Glass, Paul L. Leberg, Thomas C. Michot, and William J. Vermillion. We thank Michael T. Green and Tara S. Zimmerman for their support, guidance and editorial advice. We thank Geoff Sanders for assistance in data compilation. We thank Elizabeth Cruz, National Wildlife Refuge System, Pacific Region, Portland, Oregon for assistance in development of figures. We thank David Blankinship, Jenny Hoskins, William H. Howe, William J. Vermillion, and a number of anonymous reviewers for their helpful suggestions on earlier drafts and particularly Kimball L. Garrett for many insightful discussions, help with literature references and suggestions on an earlier draft of the manuscript. We thank Patricia Worthing for her editorial assistance. Funding for this status assessment was provided by the U.S. Fish and Wildlife Service, Regions 1, 2, 4, 6, and 8 nongame migratory bird programs.

Taxonomy

Class: Aves

Order: Charadriiformes

Family: Laridae

Scientific name: *Gelochelidon nilotica* Gmelin 1789

Common name: Gull-billed Tern

The Gull-billed Tern has a cosmopolitan but discontinuous distribution (Fig. 1) with six subspecies described based on variation in size and coloration of dorsal plumage. Two subspecies, *Gelochelidon nilotica aranea* and *G. n. vanrossemi*, occur in North America. The nominate subspecies *G. n. nilotica* breeds in small numbers in northern Germany and Denmark, and in scattered colonies across southern Europe south to northwestern Africa and east through Turkey and the Middle East to Asia Minor, India and southern Mongolia (Cramp 1985, Urban et al. 1986, Hagemeijer and Blair 1997); it winters mainly in Africa and India. Poorly differentiated from nominate birds, the subspecies *G. n. addenda* ("*G. n. affinis*" of many authors is a synonym; Dickinson 2003) breeds in coastal China and perhaps elsewhere in eastern Asia, wintering south to southeast Asia and possibly northern Australia (Higgins and Davies 1996, Wells 1999). Australian breeding birds are the largest and palest subspecies, *G. n. macrotarsa* (Higgins and Davies 1996). *G. n. groenvoldi* breeds locally in eastern South America from Brazil to northern Argentina (Blake 1977). The subspecific identity of breeding birds in southwestern Ecuador is unknown, though measurements are consistent with the subspecies *G. n. aranea* (Ridgely and Greenfield 2001).

Figure 1. North American distribution of the Gull-billed Tern.

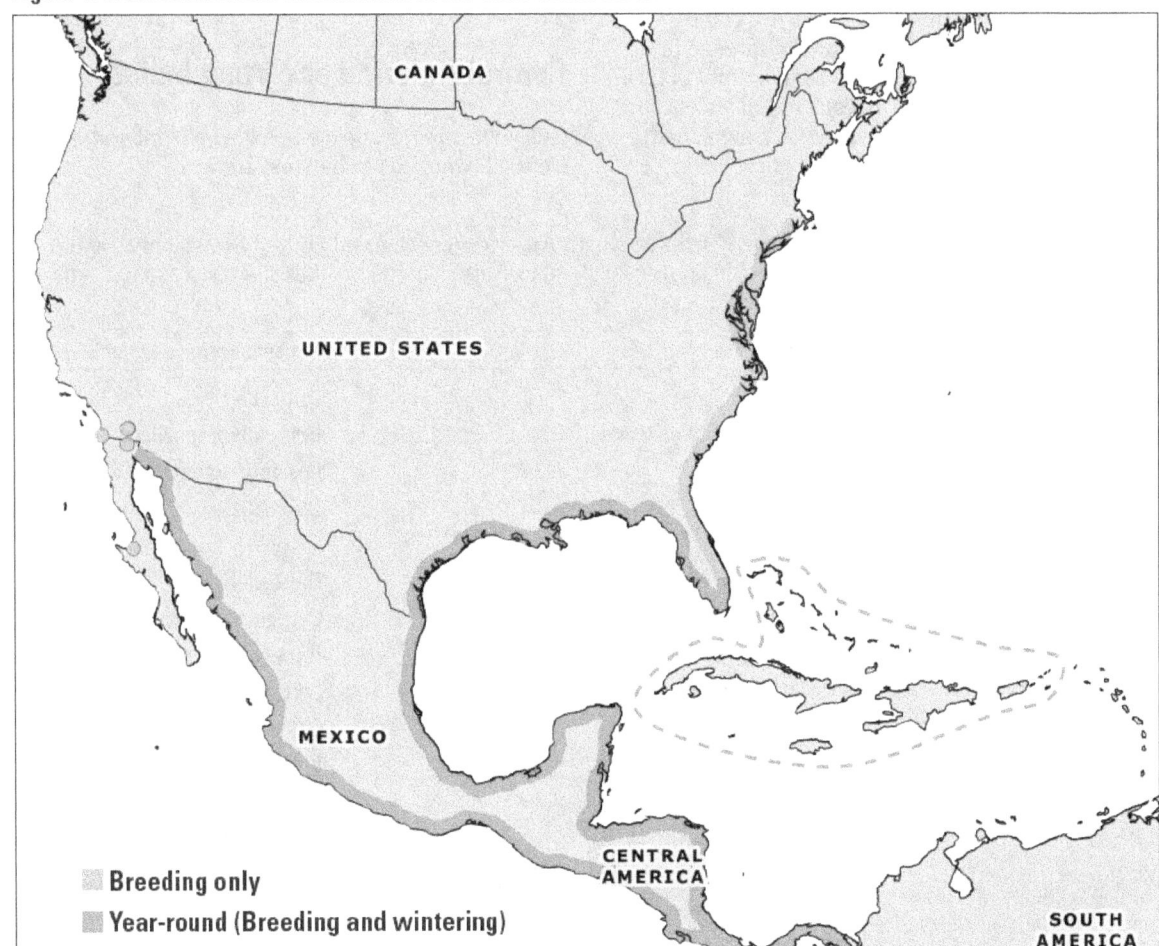

■ Breeding only

■ Year-round (Breeding and wintering)

Legal Status

United States

Gull-billed Terns are federally protected by the Migratory Bird Treaty Act (1918) (MBTA) in the United States (16 U.S.C. 703-712; Ch. 128; July 13, 1918; 40 Stat. 755). The MBTA is the primary federal law that implements international treaties mandating the conservation and management of migratory birds jointly with Great Britain, Mexico, Japan, and Russia (16 U.S.C. 703-712, as amended). The species is listed by the U.S. Fish and Wildlife Service (USFWS) as a Bird of Conservation Concern at the national scale and in four USFWS Regions (Regions 2, 4, 5, and 8) and seven Bird Conservation Regions (BCRs 27, 30, 31, 32, 33, 36, and 37) (U.S. Fish and Wildlife Service 2008). These designations identify Gull-billed Terns as a species in need of conservation.

At the state level, Gull-billed Terns are listed as Endangered in Maryland and Threatened in Georgia, North Carolina, and Virginia (Table 1). It is a Species of Special Concern or equivalent in Alabama, California, Louisiana, Mississippi, and South Carolina, but has no specific conservation status in the remaining five states in its range (Appendices A and B). The National Heritage Status ranking for Gull-billed Terns is "Critically Imperiled" or "Imperiled" in 10 of the 14 states in its range (Table 1). The National Conservation status of Gull-billed Terns in the United States is "Apparently Secure" and its Global Heritage Status is "Secure" (NatureServe Explorer 2006).

Mexico

Gull-billed Terns are protected under the 1936 Convention between the United States and Mexico for the Protection of Migratory Birds and Game Mammals, but have no special legal status in Mexico (Secretaría de Medio Ambiente y Recursos Naturales 2002).

Central America and West Indies

Gull-billed Terns appear to have no legal status in Central America or the West Indies.

Table 1. State agency status of Gull-billed Terns in North America (continental United States only), and National Heritage Status (NatureServe Explorer 2006). "No status" indicates that the state has not it given the species a specific conservation status.

State	Legal Status	National Heritage Status
Alabama	Protected	Imperiled
California	Species of special concern	Critically imperiled
Delaware	No status	Possibly extirpated
Florida	No status	Imperiled
Georgia	Threatened	Critically imperiled
Louisiana	Rare animal of conservation concern	Imperiled
Maryland	Endangered	Critically imperiled
Mississippi	Species of greatest conservation need	Imperiled
New Jersey	No status	Critically imperiled
New York	No status	Critically imperiled
North Carolina	Threatened	Vulnerable
South Carolina	Species of concern	Unranked
Texas	No status	Apparently secure
Virginia	Threatened	Imperiled

Description

Gull-billed Terns are a medium-sized (35 cm, 170–190 g) member of the Sterninae sub-family, best distinguished by the combination of its heavy black bill, black legs, and very pale gray upperparts. Compared to other medium-sized terns, it is longer-legged, has broader-based wings with longer outer primaries, and a shorter tail with a shallower fork. The following plumage information has been taken from Cramp (1985), Parnell et al. (1995), Sibley (2000), and from specimens at the University of California at Los Angeles Dickey Bird and Mammal Collection and the Natural History Museum of Los Angeles County.

Alternate-plumaged adults have a jet black crown, are white on the head and underparts, and very pale gray on the back, upperwings, rump, and tail. In basic plumage, adults lose the black cap and appear white-headed with a small dark gray patch behind the eye and indistinct black peppering on the crown. At fledging, juveniles show a buffy wash and interior brown markings on the back feathers and wing coverts, dark markings on the tertials and rectrices, and extensively dusky primaries. The crown of juveniles is whitish with fine dark spotting, and the patch behind the eye is gray. First alternate (one year old) birds resemble basic-plumaged adults but show some dark in the centers of the tertials and may show some black mottling on the center and rear of the crown. Second winter birds are essentially indistinguishable from basic-plumaged adults but differ subtly in molt limits and wear in the flight feathers. Second summer birds closely resemble alternate-plumaged adults but usually retain some white on the forehead.

The two North American subspecies (*G. n. aranea* and *G. n. vanrossemi*) are, on average, morphologically distinct, with *G. n. vanrossemi* bigger overall. There is substantial overlap in most characteristics making it difficult to distinguish between the two subspecies (Parnell et al. 1995, Molina and Erwin 2006).

Kathy Molina©

Geographic Distribution

Breeding

Gelochelidon nilotica aranea.—G. n. aranea breeds along the Atlantic coast of the United States from Long Island, New York, south to northeastern Florida and locally in the interior of Florida (Fig. 1). Along the Gulf of Mexico coast, *G. n. aranea* breeds from Tampa Bay, Florida, west through coastal Alabama, Mississippi, and Louisiana to Texas and south to Tamaulipas (Garza-Torres and Navarro S. 2003) and possibly Veracruz, Mexico (Fig. 1; Parnell et al. 1995). Gull-billed Terns were absent along the eastern coast of Yucatan, Mexico in 1992 (Rangel-Salazar et al. 1993). Although their status and distribution in the Caribbean is poorly known, *G. n. aranea* is thought to breed sporadically and in small numbers on Caribbean islands from the Bahamas south to the British Virgin Islands and Anguilla (Chardine et al. 2000).

*Gelochelidon nilotica vanrossemi.—*In the western United States, G. *n. vanrossemi* breeds very locally in extreme southern California at San Diego Bay and at the Salton Sea (Fig. 1). In western Mexico, *G. n. vanrossemi* breeds in the Colorado River Delta in northeastern Baja California, as well as in coastal Sinaloa, Nayarit and Colima (Fig. 1; Palacios and Mellink 2007). *G. n. vanrossemi* has bred sparingly and infrequently at the Guerrero Negro saltworks in extreme northern Baja California Sur (Fig. 1; Danemann and Carmona 2000, Palacios and Mellink 2007).

*Subspecies undetermined.—*In Central America, Gull-billed Terns possibly breed in Panama (Ridgely and Gwynne 1989), but confirmed breeding records are lacking and the subspecific identity of possible breeders is unknown.

Wintering

Gelochelidon nilotica aranea.—G. n. aranea winters south of the central Atlantic coast of Florida, along the Gulf of Mexico coasts from Louisiana to the Lower Laguna Madre, in Texas, and possibly along the coasts of Tamaulipas and Veracruz in Mexico (Fig. 1). Howell and Webb (1995) suggest that the species occurs in winter along the entire Gulf of Mexico and Caribbean coastlines of Mexico, Belize (where uncommon; Jones 2003) and Honduras. Documentation indicates that a few birds winter in coastal Yucatan, Mexico (Gómez de Silva 2007).

Matt Sadowski©

Gelochelidon nilotica vanrossemi.—*G. n. vanrossemi* primarily winters in Mexico along the eastern Gulf of California from the Colorado River Delta south to Sinaloa and along the Pacific coast to Nayarit, Colima and Oaxaca (Howell and Webb 1995). There are a few mid-winter records for the Salton Sea (Patten et al. 2003), the Mexicali Valley (R. A. Erickson, pers. comm.), and southern Baja California Sur (Fig. 1; Erickson et al. 2003).

Subspecies undetermined.—The non-breeding distribution of G. *n. aranea* and G. *n. vanrossemi* from southern Mexico to northern South America is poorly understood. Gull-billed Terns winter in small numbers on both coasts of Honduras (Monroe 1968), Costa Rica (Stiles and Skutch 1989) and Panama (Ridgely and Gwynne 1989). Although it is likely that migrant and wintering Gull-billed Terns on the Caribbean coast of Central and South America belong to the subspecies G. *n. aranea,* the subspecific identity of birds wintering on the southern Pacific Coast is unclear (Molina and Erwin 2006). The single specimen from the Pacific coast of Honduras appears from measurements to be G. *n. aranea* (Monroe 1968), so some Gull-billed Terns on the Pacific coast of Central and South America may be of this subspecies. The pattern of eastern North American and Caribbean breeding populations wintering on the southern Pacific Coast occurs in other avian taxa (Molina and Erwin 2006).

Migration and Vagrancy

Gelochelidon nilotica aranea.—*G. n. aranea* migrates through coastal areas of the Atlantic states and Gulf of Mexico. Migrants may be noted away from known breeding sites but normally occur within the general breeding range of the species. Small numbers may disperse northward as vagrants in spring, summer, and fall. Gull-billed Terns occur nearly annually in Massachusetts from May to September (Veit and Petersen 1993) and have been recorded in the Canadian Maritime Provinces in July and August (Godfrey 1986). Gull-billed Terns are casual or accidental in the interior of eastern North America (McWilliams and Brauning 2000). Correa-Sandoval and Garcia-Barron (1993) considered the Gull-billed Tern to be a rare migrant in the large lagoon systems of Campeche and Yucatan, Mexico.

Gelochelidon nilotica vanrossemi.—*G. n. vanrossemi* migrates along the western coast of mainland Mexico and presumably the Pacific and Gulf of California coasts of the Baja Peninsula (Wilbur 1987, Erickson et al. 2001, 2004). Gull-billed Terns are casual or accidental in the interior of western North America (Monson and Phillips 1981), including interior southern California (Lehman 1994, Hamilton and Willick 1996; McCaskie and Garrett 2001, 2004, 2005).

Summer Non-breeding

Small numbers of both subspecies over-summer within the respective portions of their winter ranges in Mexico (Howell and Webb 1995). Contreras-Balderas (1993) considered *G. n. aranea* as a year-round resident in Tamaulipas. In California, non-breeders (white-headed birds presumably in their second year) have been noted at breeding colonies at the Salton Sea (KCM).

Kathy Molina©

Natural History

Breeding

Colonies, nests, and nest spacing.—Gull-billed Tern nesting colonies are generally small to medium in size (< 50 pairs) and are loosely aggregated (Parnell et al. 1995). In Texas, 90% of 136 colony sites in 2003 contained a median of one to 50 pairs, eight sites (6%) contained 51 to 100 pairs, and six sites (4%) contained > 100 pairs. At the Salton Sea in California, Gull-billed Terns often form subcolonies of 10 to 30 pairs (KCM). Nests are small shallow scrapes typically containing little or no nest lining. Nest rims are composed of small bits of beach debris, (e.g. vegetation, small fish bones, bits of plastic, pebbles, and feathers). Both members of the pair participate in forming and maintaining the nest scrape and rim (Cramp 1985, Parnell et al. 1995). Inter-nest distances vary from 0.3 to 20 m (Gochfeld and Burger 1996).

Reproductive phenology.—The following breeding information has been taken from Parnell et al. (1995), except where noted. In California, Gull-billed Terns generally arrive in mid-March to early April, but may arrive as early as the first week of March at the Salton Sea. Egg laying usually begins by mid-April to early May in California and Baja California (Molina and Garrett 2001) and is presumed to be the same in western Mexico. Nesting by Gull-billed Terns at the Salton Sea may occur as late as mid-July through early August and is presumed to involve re-nesting attempts. In Atlantic Coast colonies, most egg laying begins from mid-May to early June. Both sexes participate in incubation, a period lasting 21-23 days beginning with the first egg. Earliest hatching is in early May in the west; most hatching on the Atlantic Coast occurs in June (Eyler et al. 1999). Chicks may move away from the nest soon after hatching, depending on the degree of disturbance and vegetation around nest sites. In extreme heat, parents lead very young broods to loafing areas at the water's edge (KCM). First flights occur at 28–35 days. Young are fed by both parents at least four weeks post-fledging.

Breeding site fidelity.—Breeding site fidelity of Gull-billed Terns has been reported to be weak in Virginia (Erwin et al. 1998b) and Europe (Cramp 1985, Parnell et al. 1995). On the Pacific Coast, Gull-billed Terns often occupy colony sites for multiple years. They nested for five and 10 consecutive years at two sites at the Salton Sea (Molina 2004), 11 consecutive years (except 2000) at San Diego Bay (R. T. Patton, pers. comm.), and since 1996 at Cerro

Prieto, Mexico, although some years were not surveyed (Molina and Garrett 2001, KCM). Reasons for the difference in site-fidelity are unknown, but could be in response to the number of alternative sites or to management aimed at reducing disturbance and predation events in California (KCM).

Demography and limiting factors.—Few quantitative data are available on the demography of Gull-billed Tern populations in North America (Parnell et al. 1995). The average clutch size ranges from two to three eggs, with four eggs being exceptional (Bent 1921). In Virginia, from 1994 through 1996, clutch size depended strongly on time of season; early clutches averaged 2.47 and late ones averaged 2.10 (n = 428; Eyler et al. 1999). In California, clutch size in 1993 averaged 2.2 (n = 140; Parnell et al. 1995). The age of first breeding in Europe has been reported to be at least five years, with birds establishing non-nesting territories at four years of age (Moller 1975). At the Salton Sea, a few known-age birds have bred at three years and occasionally birds presumed to be two years of age loaf at colony sites (KCM).

Productivity estimates vary among years and locations, and lack of consistency in the variables measured often confound comparisons of reproductive success across studies. In Virginia from 1994 to 1996, Eyler et al. (1999) reported a mean brood size of 1.99 chicks, but only 0.89 chicks per successfully hatched nest reached fledging age. For all nests initiated, including those lost to flooding or other causes, 0.53 chicks per nest survived to fledging age. In California, fledglings per pair in 2000 and 2001 for Salton Sea colonies were 0.57 and 0.31, respectively, and for the San Diego colony were 1.23 and 0.95, respectively (KCM).

Although Gull-billed Terns generally have only one brood in a breeding season, they may re-nest if the initial clutch or brood is lost (Parnell et al. 1995). No information on lifetime reproductive success is available; similarly, information on the longevity of Gull-billed Terns is scant. One bird banded as a chick in South Carolina was recovered in Guyana, South America when at least six years and four months old (Clapp et al. 1982). In Europe, the longevity record is 15 years, 10 months (Rydzewski 1978). Several 10-year old birds, banded as chicks at the Salton Sea, have been observed in the vicinity of their natal colonies (KCM).

Predators.—Known predators of eggs or chicks of Gull-billed Terns in North America are raccoons (*Procyon lotor*), coyotes (*Canis latrans*), feral dogs (*C. lupus familiaris*) and cats (*Felis catus*), rats (*Rattus* spp.), Peregrine Falcons (*Falco peregrinus*), Laughing (*Larus atricilla*), California (*L. californicus*), Herring (*L. argentatus)* and Great Black-backed (*L. marinus*) gulls, Burrowing (*Athene cunicularia*) and Great Horned (*Bubo virginianus*) owls, and ghost crabs (*Ocypode quadrata*) (Blus and Stafford 1980, Parnell et al. 1995, Eyler et al. 1999, O'Connell and Beck 2003). Other potential predators of eggs or chicks could be red foxes (*Vulpes vulpes*), skunks (*Spilogale putorius* and *Mephitis mephitis)*, ground squirrels (*Spermophilus* spp.), Western (*L. occidentalis*), Yellow-footed (*L. livens*) and Heermann's (*L. heermanni*) gulls, large herons (Ardeidae), American Kestrels (*F. sparverius*), Common Ravens (*Corvus corax*), and American Crows (*C. brachyrhynchos*) (Parnell et al. 1995, Gonzalez-Bernal et al. 2003).

Diet.—The diet of Gull-billed Terns, composed of vertebrate and invertebrate prey, is broader than most other species of terns. They are opportunistic feeders on a variety of terrestrial and aquatic animals; invertebrate prey of terrestrial and aquatic origin appears to dominate their diets. At San Diego Bay, small marine invertebrates, primarily mole crabs (*Emerita analoga*), and small fish were the dominant prey items delivered by adults to chicks, comprising 43% and 25%, respectively, of all deliveries observed in 2002 (Molina and Marschalek 2003). Additional diet items included common side-blotched (*Uta stansburiana)* and western fence (*Sceloporus occidentalis*) lizards, insects, and small chicks of Black-necked Stilts (*Himantopus mexicanus*), Killdeer (*Charadrius vociferous*), western Snowy Plovers (*C. alexandrinus nivosus*), and California Least Terns (*Sternula antillarum browni*). At the Salton Sea, 49% of prey items delivered to chicks in 2001 were insects [orthopterans (mainly crickets), odonates, and hymenoptera], with small fish (*Tilapia*) comprising 41% (KCM). Other food items delivered, listed in descending order of importance, were amphibians, crayfish, and small Black-necked Stilt chicks. Additional prey items taken at the Salton Sea include common side-blotched lizards and periodically abundant insects such as cicadas, butterflies, weevils, and ladybird beetles. In the Gulf of California and mainland Mexico, Gull-billed Terns feed on fiddler crabs (*Uca* spp.) and farmed shrimp (KCM). In Virginia, small marine invertebrates (primarily fiddler crabs), fish, and insects (primarily large odonates and orthopterans) were the dominant prey items fed to chicks in 1995 and 1996 (Erwin et al. 1998a). In Lavaca Bay, Texas, Quinn and Wiggins (1990) reported that 47.5% of prey

delivered to chicks in 1981 consisted of terrestrial orthopterans, arachnids, and assorted insects, while the remaining prey items were associated with marine (shrimp, crabs, and fish) or fresh or brackish water (odonates and frogs) habitats. In Louisiana, Gull-billed Terns feed on crayfish at Lake Charles in winter (Clement 1946).

Foraging Behavior

The following is from Parnell et al. (1995), except where noted. By virtue of their varied diet and their habit of exploiting insect and lizard prey in terrestrial habitats, Gull-billed Terns forage over a wide range of substrates. In terrestrial and aquatic habitats, Gull-billed Terns forage on the wing, with characteristic buoyant swoops down to the substrate to pluck prey from the surface or near surface. They may frequently hover over the surface when foraging into the wind. Aerial prey (swarming insects such as weevils or ladybird beetles) is taken directly from the air column. Unlike other terns, Gull-billed Terns rarely, if ever, plunge-dive for prey. Gull-billed Terns usually swallow small items in flight but may land to manipulate or disarticulate larger items (Molina and Marschalek 2003). Both parents feed young, although the relative contributions of the sexes have not been quantified.

Gull-billed Terns are known to kleptoparasitize breeding Black Skimmers (*Rynchops niger*) in Texas (D. J. Newstead, pers. comm.), Common Terns (*Sterna hirundo*) in New Jersey (Parnell et al. 1995), and occasionally California Least and Forster's terns (*S. forsteri*) in California (Molina and Marschelek 2003, B. E. Collins, pers. comm.).

Pemberton (1922) reported foraging distances of up to 22.5 km from Gull-billed Tern nesting colonies in Texas. Regular foraging distances of up to 9 km away from the nesting colony occurred in San Diego Bay (Molina and Marschelek (2003). Gull-billed Terns were observed foraging in areas up to 76 km north of the San Diego Bay nesting colony (B. Foster, pers. comm.), but it is unknown if these birds were active breeders.

Post-breeding Dispersal

Gull-billed Terns gather in small groups at river deltas, estuaries, sandy beaches, flooded agricultural fields, and inundated salt flats after young fledge. In California and Baja California, post-breeding movement may begin as early as mid-July with most, if not all, birds leaving breeding areas by mid- to late August (Parnell et al. 1995). Along the Atlantic Coast, Gull-billed Terns are one of the earliest of the terns to disperse from breeding colonies, often as early as late July (RME).

Population Estimates and Trends

Gull-billed Terns are not considered to be abundant anywhere in their North American range (Parnell et al. 1995, Gochfeld and Burger 1996). There are few historical population estimates for either subspecies in North America, especially for Mexico. When state census data are available, they often have not been collected simultaneously throughout an entire region. We compiled published and unpublished results of surveys conducted throughout the U.S. and western Mexico to gain a more complete and updated understanding of current population levels for both subspecies in North America over the last two decades.

Estimates

Spendelow and Patton (1988) estimated 5400 Gull-billed Terns for the entire U.S. from 1976 to 1982, which when converted using Erwin's (1979) pairs-to-adults conversion factor of 0.66, yields 3563 pairs. This estimate excluded birds in California (Spendelow and Patton 1988) and may underestimate the population in Florida (Parnell et al. 1995); thus underestimating the entire U.S. population.

Gelochelidon nilotica aranea.—For the southeastern U.S. (excluding Virginia and the Florida Gulf of Mexico coasts), Clapp et al. (1983) reported 3472 Gull-billed Terns from 1972 to 1979. For ease of comparison, we use Erwin's (1979) pairs-to-adults conversion factor to convert Clapp et al.'s (1983) estimate of individuals into 2292 pairs. Portnoy et al. (1981) estimated 1314 Gull-billed Terns in North Carolina south to Atlantic Florida; Kress et al. (1983) equated this figure to 650 pairs. Clapp and Buckley (1984) estimated a total of 3019 pairs of Gull-billed Terns along the southern Atlantic and Gulf of Mexico coasts between 1976 and 1983. For the north and mid-Atlantic Coast in 1982, Buckley and Buckley (1984) reported a probable 1000 pairs; yielding 4019 pairs for the entire eastern U.S. when combined with Clapp and Buckley's (1984) total. In summary, population estimates for the *G. n. aranea* subspecies in the U.S. from 1976 to 1983 ranged from about 3563 to 4019 pairs.

The lack of systematic survey efforts in all states with *G. n. aranea* colonies makes it difficult to compare recent population sizes with those reported above and difficult to account for inter-annual movements. In no single year have all states with colonies been surveyed simultaneously, and during the years 2000 to 2004 most states have reported counts for only one year (Table 2). To estimate total numbers in recent years (2000–2004), we summed the mean counts for all states with breeding colonies and the highest count for each state during this period (Table 2). The resulting population estimates for *G. n. aranea* for 2000–2004 are 3608 pairs (sum of mean counts) and 4432 pairs (sum of high counts).

Although Gull-billed Terns are known to breed in the large lagoon system of Laguna Madre in Tamaulipas, Mexico (Garza-Torres and Navarro S. 2003), no historic or recent population estimates are available. A preliminary survey in 2005 in the state of Veracruz did not locate active colony sites (EM); no other comprehensive survey in Mexico has been conducted.

Gelochelidon nilotica vanrossemi.—The earliest available assessment of the historical population size of *G. n. vanrossemi* in the U.S. is Pemberton's (1927) estimate of 500 pairs nesting at the Salton Sea's south end in 1927. By 1937, fewer than 200 pairs nested there (Grinnell and Miller 1944). This decline continued through the 1950s and 1960s with 60 pairs in 1952, 75 pairs in 1957, 40-50 pairs in 1959, and just a few pairs through the 1960s (Remsen 1978). By 1976 only 17 pairs nested at the Salton Sea (McCaskie 1976) and twice this number may have nested in 1977 (Remsen 1978). During the 1980s, the largest count reported was a minimum of 75 pairs in 1986 (McCaskie 1986).

In 1986, Gull-billed Terns colonized a single site on the California coast at the saltworks in southern San Diego Bay, which became part of the San Diego Bay National Wildlife Refuge (NWR) in 1999. This colony increased to 30 pairs in 1992, varied between eight and 20 pairs through the remainder of the 1990s, and steadily climbed from approximately 24 pairs in 2000 to 54 pairs in 2006 (R. T. Patton, pers. comm.). The species has not established colonies at any other location in coastal California or away from the Salton Sea. During the early 1990s, an average of 120 pairs of Gull-billed Terns nested at the Salton Sea and San Diego Bay NWR (Clapp et al. 1993, Parnell et al. 1995). From 1997 to 2004, an average of 146 pairs nested in California at these two sites (Table 3).

Table 2. Number of breeding pairs and colony sites of *G. n. aranea* in the continental United States for years in which comprehensive state-wide censuses were conducted.

Year	No. of Pairs	No. of Colonies	Avg. Pairs/ Colony	Year	No. of Pairs	No. of Colonies	Avg. Pairs/ Colony
Atlantic Coast				Mississippi (cont'd)			
New York				2003[f]	2	1	—
1977	0	0	—	2004[f]	150	1	—
1985	2	2	1	Louisiana			
1995	2	1	—	1976[d]	154	4	39
2003	11	3	4	1990[g]	161	3	54
New Jersey				1991[h]	30	1	—
1977	19	4	5	1992[h]	350	2	175
1985	17	3	5	1993[h]	650	3	217
1995	18[a]	3	6	1994[h]	290	4	73
2001	92[a]	5	18	1995[h]	400	3	133
Virginia				1996[h]	173	4	43
1977	729[a]	11	66	1997[h]	248	11	23
1984	413	11	38	1998[h]	1120	5	224
1993	265	15	18	1999[h]	590	5	118
1998	310	15	21	2001[i]	440	4	110
2003	293	16	18	Texas[j]			
North Carolina				1973[c]	2187	27	81
1977	621	21	30	1974[c]	688	17	41
1985	174	4	44	1975[c]	1289	23	56
1995	249	10	25	1976	1098	21	52
2001	258	7	37	1977	1632	32	51
South Carolina				1978	2034	30	68
1976	154[a]	4	39	1979	2267	38	60
1988	254	10	25	1980	1810	33	55
1995	165	8	21	1981	2046	39	53
2003	239	7	34	1982	2123	40	53
Georgia				1983	4661	33	141
1995	80	1	—	1984	2416	47	51
2003	54	1	—	1985	1926	42	46
Florida				1986	1075	32	34
1975	534	2	267	1987	1946	38	51
1980–1985[b]	75[c]	6–8	—	1988	1243	36	35
2000	17	3	6	1989	1150	40	29
Gulf Coast				1990	2868	37	78
Alabama				1991	913	21	44
1976[d]	23	1	—	1992	1372	35	39
2001[e]	87	3	29	1993	1553	34	46
2002[e]	50	1	—	1994	3706	41	90
2003[e]	9	1	—	1995	2553	28	91
2004[e]	85	3	28	1996	914	37	25
Mississippi				1997	1576	36	44
1976[d]	2	1	—	1998	2293	41	56
1994[f]	0	0	—	1999	846	29	19
1995[f]	0	0	—	2000	2791	39	72
1996[f]	2	1	—	2001	1840	36	51
1997[f]	1	1	—	2002	2565	39	66
1998[f]	0	0	—	2003	1292	29	45
1999[f]	0	0	—				
2000[f]	0	0	—				
2001[f]	0	0	—				
2002[f]	5	1	—				

a Breeding pairs estimated from counts of individuals by multiplying individuals by 0.667.
b Smith and Alvear 1997
c Minimum estimate due to incomplete state survey coverage.
d Portnoy 1977
e R. B. Clay, pers. comm.
f M. P. Stevens, pers. comm.
g Martin and Lester 1990
h G. D. Lester, pers. comm.
i Michot et al. 2004
j U.S. Fish and Wildlife Service 2004

Table 3. Number of breeding pairs and colony sites of *G. n. vanrossemi* in the Pacific Coast of the United States and Mexico in years surveys were conducted.

Year	No. of Pairs	No. of Colonies	Avg. Pairs/ Colony
United States			
California[a]			
1992	136	4	34
1993	131	4	33
1994	113	4	28
1995	92	3	27
1996[b]	155	3	55
1997	162	3	53
1998	131–133	3	—
1999	112–122	3	—
2000	135–142	4	—
2001	173	2	87
2002[c]	97–101	2	—
2003	187–192	4	—
2004	157	2	79
2005	252–257	5	—
Mexico[d,e]			
Baja California			
2003	183	2	92
2004	234	2	—
2005	274	2	137
Baja California Sur			
2003	14	1	—
2005	10	1	—
Sonora			
2003	0	0	—
2005	0	0	—
Sinaloa			
2003	15	1	—
2005	26–27	2	14
Nayarit			
2003	122–152	2	—
2005	185	2	93
Colima			
2003	15	1	—
2005	55	5	11

a Data for Salton Sea: 1992 to 2001 from Molina 2004; 2002 to 2005 from KCM. Data for San Diego: 1992 to 2005 from R. T. Patton, pers. comm.

b Data from Salton Sea colonies only.

c Data from San Diego and some Salton Sea colonies.

d Data from Palacios and Mellink 2007, except Baja California (2004) from KCM.

e Palacios and Mellink 2007 also surveyed Jalisco, Michoacán, Guerrero, Oaxaca, and Chiapas but reported no breeding.

Historical estimates of Gull-billed Terns breeding along the Pacific coast of Mexico are unavailable. A total of 367 potential nesting sites were surveyed in 2003, with an estimated total of 376 nesting pairs of Gull-billed Terns distributed among seven colonies in western Mexico (EM, EP). In 2005, Palacios and Mellink (2007) and KCM documented 550 to 551 breeding pairs among six of the seven breeding locations documented in 2003 and at one additional site. Combined with the number of pairs in California, 737 to 808 pairs of *G. n. vanrossemi* appear to have nested in western North America in 2003 and 2005 (Table 3).

Trends

Gelochelidon nilotica aranea.—The numbers of breeding Gull-billed Terns along the northern Atlantic coast are small, but seem to be stable or increasing slightly, while numbers along the mid- and southern Atlantic coasts have declined since the mid- to late 1970s (Table 2). In Virginia, partial surveys in 1975 and 1976 recorded high totals of 1485 and 1333 pairs, respectively, and a complete survey in 1977 recorded 729 pairs (Brinker et al. 2007, 2008). In North Carolina, declines occurred between 1975 and 1976 and the mid-1980s, with numbers remaining at about a third of the state's mid-1970s levels (D. H. Allen, pers. comm.). In Florida, a relatively large number of breeding Gull-billed Terns (534 pairs in 1975) appeared to have dwindled to just a few pairs, although comprehensive surveys of the state have been infrequent (Table 2; Smith and Alvear 1997). The number of pairs in South Carolina appears to be stable or increasing slightly, while the population in Georgia may be declining (Table 2). In Maryland and Delaware, the species is possibly extirpated. The number of pairs breeding in Delaware has historically been small, and no breeding has been documented since 1991 (D. B. Carter, pers. comm.). The number of pairs in Alabama, Mississippi, and Louisiana are small, but apparently stable or increasing slightly (Table 2; Portnoy 1977, R. B. Clay and M. P. Stevens, pers. comm.). In Texas, where the largest known breeding concentrations in North America occur, Gull-billed Tern numbers appear to have remained stable overall since the early 1970s (Table 2).

Gelochelidon nilotica vanrossemi.—Although declines were apparent from the late 1930s through the late 1970s at the Salton Sea, the small number of breeding pairs in California seems to have remained stable since the early 1990s (Table 3; KCM). In 1986, Gull-billed Terns increased their numbers slightly by colonizing one coastal site at San Diego Bay. No trend information is available for Mexico (KCM).

Monitoring Activities

Breeding Bird Survey

The Breeding Bird Survey (Sauer et al. 2008) does not adequately monitor this species because survey routes do not adequately represent Gull-billed Tern breeding areas in coastal estuarine habitats (KCM). Gull-billed Terns were not included in Breeding Bird Survey trend analysis by Price et al. (1995).

Regional and State Surveys

There are no coordinated breeding or winter surveys of Gull-billed Terns throughout their entire range in the United States or in North America. The Gulf of Mexico coasts of Alabama, Mississippi, and Louisiana were occasionally surveyed as a region; this survey was last conducted in 1976 (Portnoy 1977). Known Gull-billed Tern colony sites are monitored annually in California and Virginia (RME, KCM). In Texas, Mississippi, Alabama, South Carolina, and New York, Gull-billed Tern colonies are monitored annually as part of each state's comprehensive waterbird nesting surveys (P. Glass, M. P. Stevens, R. B. Clay, T. M. Murphy, and M. R. Wasilco, pers. comm.). Louisiana conducts comprehensive surveys of nesting waterbirds at least every four years (P. L. Leberg, pers. comm.),

and may include Gull-billed Terns. New Jersey, North Carolina, and Georgia conduct periodic surveys of breeding waterbird colonies including Gull-billed Terns (C. D. Jenkins, S. E. Cameron, and J. S. Calver, pers. comm.). In Florida, the only monitoring efforts conducted recently for Gull-billed Terns were those directed toward the state breeding bird atlas (J. A. Rodgers, pers. comm.). State breeding bird atlases documenting Gull-billed Tern colonies were published for New York (Bull 1964), New Jersey (Walsh et al. 1999), Maryland (Brinker 1996), Mississippi (Gandy and Turcotte 1970), and Louisiana (Michot et al. 2004), and an atlas is currently under development in Alabama (KCM). A preliminary survey in the state of Veracruz in Mexico in 2005 yielded no colony sites (EM). Comprehensive surveys in coastal eastern Mexico for *G. n. aranea* have not been conducted.

To facilitate coordinated comprehensive survey efforts, the USFWS sponsored the development of field identification cards (in English and Spanish) and a bi-national workshop in 2003 to address a standardized survey protocol for *G. n. vanrossemi*. The USFWS also sponsored the first comprehensive surveys for *G. n. vanrossemi* in Mexico in 2003 and 2005, which combined with annual monitoring in California, resulted in the first range-wide surveys for this subspecies.

Matt Sadowski©

Habitat Requirements

Breeding Season

In North America, Gull-billed Terns typically nest on barrier islands, dredged-material islands, constructed islets or isolated levees in wildlife, salt extraction, and aquaculture impoundments, shell bars and islands in open marshes, abandoned causeways, natural islets in shallow tidal and brackish lagoons, and sand and shellbars in river deltas (Parnell et al. 1995). Nesting substrates include bare sand, gravel, crushed shell, and silty clay soils. Nest sites generally lack vegetation, but when present, it is usually low and sparse. In Texas, Gull-billed Terns have nested in dense areas of the grasses *Paspalum* and *Monanthochloe* (J. K. Wilson, pers. comm.) and in Virginia, the largest colony is on wrack (drifted rafts of dead *Spartina*) on a low island in a salt marsh. In western Mexico, Gull-billed Terns nest on low islands with mangrove or cactus and on mud flats with salt marsh vegetation. Gull-billed Terns have occasionally nested on gravel rooftops in coastal Texas (P. Glass, pers. comm.), Louisiana (Purrington 2002), and Florida (Coburn 1996).

Inland, nesting occurs on natural and constructed islands in saline and freshwater lakes, reservoirs, and impoundments, and on abandoned oil and gas causeways (Parnell et al. 1995, Molina and Garrett 2001, Molina 2004). In Florida, Gull-billed Terns have nested on sand fill in phosphate mine pits (Smith and Gore 1996). In the Mexican Central Plateau, one or two pairs (of either subspecies) have been observed nesting above 2200 m elevation at Lake Xochimilco and Lake Texcoco; these are the only North American breeding records significantly above sea level (Molina and Erwin 2006).

Whether on the coast or inland, colony sites are typically located near optimal foraging habitats, which include the shallow margins of bays, rivers, and marshes, exposed mudflats, the tidal margins of sandy beaches, agricultural fields and drains, wildlife, salt extraction, and aquaculture impoundments, sandy lake shores, and open shrublands.

Kathy Molina©

Winter and Summer Non-breeding Seasons

Wintering Gull-billed Terns along the Gulf of Mexico Coast are generally found in estuaries, salt and freshwater marshes, canals, and ponds. Away from the coast, this species is commonly observed in flooded agricultural fields (rice and crayfish impoundments). In western Mexico, Gull-billed Terns are usually found in bays and estuaries with extensive tidal flats, agricultural fields, canals and drains, salinas (salt mines), and aquaculture (primarily shrimp) impoundments (KCM) and use exposed dikes for courtship displays (EP). Away from the coastal lowlands on the Pacific Coast, small numbers of Gull-billed Terns are regularly found in winter near Laguna Sayula in Jalisco, an ephemeral wetland at the extreme southwest corner of the Mexican Plateau (Howell 1999).

Threats

Habitat Loss and Degradation

Vegetation succession and erosion can alter the suitability of colony sites on dredged-material islands along the Gulf of Mexico (Chaney et al. 1978) and Atlantic coasts (Parnell and Soots 1979). Changes in the distribution of ground-nesting waterbirds from 1977 to 1995 in New Jersey, Virginia, and North Carolina coincided with changes in dredging policy along the mid-Atlantic (Erwin et al. 2003). Since the 1980s, competing demands by coastal communities for sand augmentation for beaches has slowed the rate of replenishment of dredged-material islands allowing the establishment of dense and woody vegetation or the erosion and disappearance of former colony sites (Erwin et al. 2003). In North Carolina, the number of Gull-billed Terns nesting on dredged-material islands declined from 524 pairs in 1977 to only 128 pairs in 1995 (Erwin et al. 2003). Parnell et al. (1997) attributed the low nesting site fidelity and high rates of site turnover exhibited by Gull-billed Terns in North Carolina from 1977 to 1995 to the degradation of colony sites due to vegetation succession and erosion.

Increases in predator populations on Atlantic Coast barrier islands are believed responsible for the diminished suitability of these sites for Gull-billed Terns and other colonial ground nesting birds since the 1980s, especially in Virginia (Erwin et al. 2001, 2003) where, although the number of colonies has increased, the size of each and the overall number of breeding Gull-billed Terns has declined (Erwin et al. 2003). Fragmentation of larger colonies into more numerous but smaller ones does not necessarily increase successful reproduction as smaller colonies may be less resistant or resilient to predation and human disturbances (Sears 1979, Wittenberger and Hunt 1985).

Diminishing freshwater and agricultural inflows to the Salton Sea have resulted in lower water levels and the bridging of once isolated islands, rendering them accessible to mammalian predators and unsuitable for nesting. Water levels may be reduced even further by conservation measures under the Imperial Irrigation District's water transfer program (J. A. Bartel, pers. comm.).

Nesting attempts by Gull-billed Terns at Isla Montague in Mexico were consistently interrupted by regular tidal inundations throughout the 1993 and 1994 breeding seasons (Peresbarbosa and Mellink 2001). During the 2004 and 2005 breeding seasons, complete colony failures were attributed to non-storm related tidal inundations (KCM). Since the completion of upstream dams and diversions on the Colorado River in the 1930s and 1940s, this estuary island no longer receives the sediment load that prevailed prior to the damming of the river. Lacking such sediment replenishment, it is subjected to the erosion forces of Gulf of California tides (Alvarez-Borrego 2001).

The recent large scale conversion of estuarine habitats to commercial aquaculture (shrimp and oyster farms) in northwestern mainland Mexico (Páez-Osuna et al. 2003) may reduce or degrade available mudflats for foraging, while providing novel and concentrated food sources during the breeding season (Molina et al. 2009). Shrimp are generally harvested in the fall and winter, removing this food source for wintering Gull-billed Terns (Molina et al. 2009). Since 1989, the extent of wetlands converted to aquaculture in Sonora has increased some 3000% to encompass nearly 7500 ha of shrimp farms; in Sinoloa, approximately 1300 ha have been dedicated to aquaculture (Instituto Tecnologico de Sonora 2004). Loss of estuarine habitat in Mexico has also occurred through the construction of marinas and other tourism-related development and saltworks (KCM).

Overutilization

Overutilization (such as egging and over-hunting) is not a known threat to Gull-billed Terns.

Disease and Predation

No information exists regarding disease or parasites (Parnell et al. 1995). Gull-billed Terns seemed unaffected by the large outbreaks of botulism, cholera, and other diseases that occurred at the Salton Sea during the 1990s (KCM).

Low reproductive success of Gull-billed Terns in Virginia is in part attributed to predation on eggs and chicks by gulls and Great Horned Owls (Eyler et al. 1999, O'Connell and Beck 2003). O'Connell and Beck (2003) reported that 77% of 133 eggs among 64 Gull-billed Tern nests in Virginia were lost to predation by Herring and Great Black-backed gulls. Nesting by Gull-billed Terns on traditional barrier island sites has become more limited in New Jersey and Virginia due to red fox and raccoon expansions (Erwin et al. 2001).

Receding water levels have caused traditional nesting sites at the Salton Sea to become increasingly accessible to mammalian predators, resulting in complete breeding failures at the Morton Bay colony in 2004 and 2005 (KCM). The colonization of the Salton Sea and subsequent breeding by California Gulls in 1996 adversely affected Gull-billed Tern nesting and fledging success (Molina 2004). From 1997 to 2001, Gull-billed Terns ceased nesting at the Obsidian Butte colony and on two islands at the Sonny Bono Salton Sea NWR while these sites were occupied by California Gulls (Molina 2004). Gull-billed Terns reoccupied the Obsidian Butte colony site in 2004 when California Gulls ceased to nest there (KCM).

Feral dogs and cats and introduced rats are also threats to colonies in or close to urban environments. At the San Diego Bay NWR, Gull-billed Terns do not nest on isolated islands, but instead occupy sites among a network of easily accessible earthen levees where an aggressive predator control program reduces mammalian predation (B. E. Collins, pers. comm.).

Inadequacy of Existing Regulatory Mechanisms

Despite the protections and status designations denoting conservation concern at the Federal, state, and BCR scale, the species has continued to show declines in recent decades in the Atlantic Coast region, particularly in Virginia, North Carolina, Maryland and Florida (Table 2; Smith and Alvear 1997, R. B. Clay, pers. comm., RME). Populations in Texas have remained large and stable despite the lack of additional regulatory measures, apparently due to the large number of dredged material nesting sites in this state (KCM).

Other Natural or Manmade Factors

Storm events and other natural disturbances.— Colony sites on the Atlantic Coast are frequently flooded by abnormally high spring tides as well as storm events, resulting in high rates of nest loss, particularly at marsh nesting sites (Erwin et al. 1998b). Major hurricanes have had dramatic adverse impacts to nesting habitats in the Gulf of Mexico, as many sites have simply disappeared (W. J. Vermillion, pers. comm.). Spring tides regularly wash out entire nesting colonies in the Gulf of California at Isla Montague in Baja California and Isla El Rancho in Sinaloa, Mexico (Peresbarbosa and Mellink 2001, X. Vega, pers. comm.). Gull-billed Terns failed to re-nest at Isla Montague and Isla El Rancho in 2004 and 2005 after late April high tides flooded first attempts (KCM).

Pesticides or other contaminants.—There is limited information available on the exposure of Gull-billed Terns to contaminants. Residue levels of DDE in 11 Gull-billed Tern eggs collected in South Carolina in 1972 ranged from 0.28 to 10.71 μg per g (wet wt.) (Blus and Stafford 1980). Two eggs from the 1972 sample containing the highest residue levels (8.75 and 10.71 μg per g) had abnormal and fragile shells. The ranges of DDE residues in Gull-billed Tern eggs from South Carolina sampled in 1974 (n =14 eggs) and in 1975 (n = 5 eggs) declined to 0.18-1.34 μg per g and 0.14-0.38 μg per g (wet wt.), respectively (Blus and Stafford 1980). The mean eggshell thickness for the 1972, 1974, and 1975 samples ranged between 0.220 mm to 0.227 mm and was not significantly different from the mean thickness of 0.228 mm for four pre-1947 Gull-billed Tern eggs (Blus and Stafford 1980). Residues of polychlorinated biphenyls, oxychlordane, dieldrin, and trans-nonachlor were low or undetectable in Gull-billed Tern eggs sampled between 1972 and 1975 (Blus and Stafford 1980).

The geometric mean concentration of selenium for six Gull-billed Terns eggs collected from the Salton Sea in 1991 was 4.10 ppm (dry wt., range = 3.4 to 5.3; D. J. Audet, pers. comm.) below the threshold for lowered egg hatchability (Skorupa and Ohlendorf 1991). The concentration of total DDT from one Gull-billed Tern egg from San Diego Bay, California was considered elevated at 2.9 ppm (wet wt.), but below levels associated with reproductive impairment in other species (C. A. Roberts, pers. comm.). 2.9 ppm of DDT is approaching levels of severe effects in sensitive species (Blus 1984). The total PCB concentration in that egg was below the 2.9 ppm threshold at 1.8 ppm (wet wt.; C. A. Roberts, pers. comm.). Concentrations of arsenic, cadmium, chromium, copper, mercury, nickel, and zinc in the San Diego egg were below threshold levels (C. A. Roberts, pers. comm.).

The April 20, 2010 Deepwater oil rig disaster off the Louisiana coast dramatically demonstrated the actual and potential impacts of oil contamination on a wide range of coastal waterbirds, including Gull-billed Terns. Although they are less dependent on prey from marine and estuarine waters than other tern species, Gull-billed Terns along northern and eastern Gulf Coast, Florida, and the southeast Atlantic barrier islands are certainly at risk from oil-contaminated sand and marsh nesting and feeding habitats.

Population size and colony distribution.—The small population size and the low number and sizes of Gull-billed Tern breeding colonies in North America increases their vulnerability to catastrophic habitat change, human disturbances, flooding events, predation, displacement by other nesting species, and other natural and anthropogenic threats.

This is particularly true for *G. n. vanrossemi*, for which recent breeding is known at only one coastal California site, one to four sites in the Salton Sea, and six to eight widely separated sites in western Mexico. From 1992–2004, 65–90% of California's annual breeding population nested at the Salton Sea, indicating a high degree of population consolidation in one area (Table 3). Two other areas of consolidation occur in western Mexico, at Cerro Prieto and Isla Montague in Baja California and at Laguna Pericos in Nayarit. These few sites support a high percent of the *G. n. vanrossemi* population (KCM). *G. n. aranea* colonies are also small and localized on the Atlantic Coast with an area of consolidation from Virginia to South Carolina (RME).

Introduced species.—Predation by feral dogs and cats and introduced rats is discussed in the Disease and Predation section (above). The encroachment of invasive plants, salt cedar (*Tamarisk* spp.) and common reed (*Arundo* and *Phragmites* spp.), degrades nesting habitat at Salton Sea colonies (KCM).

Conflicts with other species.—In San Diego County, California, Gull-billed Terns have been observed to prey upon the eggs and chicks of two species listed under the Endangered Species Act (ESA), the threatened western Snowy Plover and endangered California Least Tern, since 2001 (R. T. Patton, pers. comm.). The highest number of observed predation events was in 2003, when 52 chicks of California Least Terns and western Snowy Plovers were taken. Additional predation was documented by the presence of California Least Tern chick leg bands in Gull-billed Tern nests (J. A. Bartel, pers. comm.). Not all predation events are directly observed, and more events are suspected (R. T. Patton, pers. comm.).

Between 1993 and 1995, conflicts with California Least Terns and western Snowy Plovers in southern California resulted in the lethal control of six Gull-billed Tern adults under the MBTA (T. E. Tate-Hall, pers. comm.). No additional lethal control of Gull-billed Terns in response to such conflict has been authorized or reported. Little information is currently available on the overall impact of predation by Gull-billed Terns on California Least Terns and western Snowy Plovers. Implementation of regular or long-term lethal control of Gull-billed Terns to protect California Least Terns and Snowy Plovers may affect the stability or growth of the Gull-billed Tern population in southern California.

Gull-billed Tern predation on Least Terns is not as evident in areas outside of southern California. Gull-billed Terns frequently share nesting colonies with Least Terns at Isla Montague, with no evidence of such predation (KCM). Gull-billed Terns have been noted to forage near a colony of Least Terns in Gulfport, Mississippi and predation of one chick was documented (Densmore 1990). Gull-billed Terns were observed to swoop on Least Tern chicks in Florida but capture was never observed (Smith and Gore 1996). Gull-billed Terns didn't include avian prey in their diet in Virginia (Erwin et al. 1998a).

Other interspecific interactions.—Black Skimmers have damaged and/or caused Gull-billed Tern nests to be abandoned, and were suspected of inflicting lethal lacerations to Gull-billed Tern chicks at San Diego Bay (R. T. Patton, pers. comm.). At the Salton Sea, loafing Brown (*Pelecanus occidentalis*) and American White (*P. erythrorhynchos*) pelicans caused high rates of nest loss and abandonment of several Gull-billed Tern colonies (KCM). In early spring 2007, Caspian Terns (*Hydroprogne caspia*) began nesting on islands at the Salton Sea typically used by breeding Gull-billed Terns, precluding the later arriving Gull-billed Terns from nesting (C. C. Schoneman, pers. comm.). In Virginia, competition with Herring and Great Black-backed gulls for nest sites among higher elevation habitats force Gull-billed Terns and other small larids to nest in flood prone areas (O'Connell and Beck 2003).

Aggressive anti-predator defenses of Gull-billed Tern are well known (Sears 1978, Parnell et al. 1995) and may benefit colony associates that show less aggressive defense (Pius and Leberg 1997, 1998). Black Skimmers may benefit from the aggressive nest defense of Gull-billed Terns by nesting in or near Gull-billed Tern colonies (Burger and Gochfeld 1990, Pius and Leberg 2002). In Florida, Gull-billed Terns frequently co-occupy nesting colonies with Least Terns (Smith and Gore 1996). In mixed species colonies, the smaller Least Tern may also benefit from *G. n. aranea's* aggressive response to predators.

Other conflicts.—The Gull-billed Tern's ability to use a variety of terrestrial habitats when foraging resulted in conflicts with military aircraft operations at the Naval Base, Coronado and Naval Outlying Landing Field, Imperial Beach in San Diego Bay. In 2004, two foraging adults were lethally removed near an active runway on the Naval Base; and in 2007, one adult was lethally removed at the Naval Outlying Landing Field (T. E. Tate-Hall, pers. comm.). These birds were removed under the authority of a Bird Airstrike Hazard permit under the MBTA (T. E. Tate-Hall, pers. comm.).

In Mexico, Gull-billed Terns forage extensively over commercial shrimp farms during harvest. Although lethal control of predators is not legally authorized in Mexico, it does occur (KCM); however, data on potential impacts are unavailable.

Disturbance to nesting sites.—Human disturbances, especially when frequent or prolonged, threaten reproductive success by exposing eggs and young to opportunistic predators or to lethal temperatures (Parnell et al. 1995). Gull-billed Tern chicks are highly precocial and will move long distances from the nest site, frequently over water, when disturbed repeatedly, potentially resulting in mortality from drowning or from immobilization in soft silty substrates (KCM). Human and pet disturbances at nesting colonies are potentially severe in Florida (Smith and Gore 1996) and Alabama, and are increasing in Virginia and North Carolina (Parnell et al. 1997). Management to reduce human disturbance has likely contributed to the presence, and in some cases persistence, of Gull-billed Tern colonies on NWRs and other managed state and federal lands (KCM).

Flickr/marj_k©

Management and Conservation

Habitat Management

Federal and state wildlife agencies and conservation organizations implement a variety of management actions to protect Gull-billed Tern colonies. At some colony locations, signs are posted or barriers are constructed to eliminate human disturbance. At a few colonies in Virginia, New Jersey, Texas, and California, experiments have been attempted with electric and traditional fencing to exclude mammalian predators. These efforts, and others to control the encroachment of vegetation at nest sites, have reduced threats of habitat modification and human disturbance (Smith and Gore 1996).

The Sonny Bono Salton Sea NWR manages water levels in freshwater impoundments to avoid shallow depths that allow access by mammalian predators, manages invasive vegetation (i.e., *Tamarisk*) to maintain open nesting habitat, and restricts public access to colonies to reduce human disturbance. The effectiveness of these management actions is evidenced by the early season abandonment of unmanaged colonies on adjacent private lands due to predator disturbances, and the subsequent relocation of these failed colonies to managed habitat in NWR impoundments (C. C. Schoneman, pers. comm.).

Isla Montague lies within the protective core zone of the Rio Colorado Delta Biosphere Reserve, but has no habitat management specifically directed at nesting Gull-billed Terns. Neither does Isla El Rancho, in Bahia Santa Maria, which is included in the Gulf of California Island Park System and the Santa Maria Bay Ecosystem Management Program (KCM). Sites in Nayarit and Colima also lack habitat management (EP).

Predator Management

Predator control, whether by lethal or non-lethal measures (e.g. fencing, predator relocation, etc.) can directly benefit Gull-billed Terns and other ground nesting colonial waterbirds at nearby colonies. In Virginia, control (removal) of foxes and raccoons is conducted on selected barrier islands (RME). Control of avian and mammalian predators is implemented annually at the San Diego Bay NWR for recovery of California Least Terns and western Snowy Plovers, incidentally benefiting Gull-billed Terns (B. E. Collins, pers. comm.). A mammalian predator control program is proposed to protect Gull-billed Tern colonies at the Sonny Bono Salton Sea NWR (C. C. Schoneman, pers. comm.). Currently, predator control is occurring at waterbird colonies located on private lands in the Salton Sea area (C. C. Schoneman, pers. comm.).

Chain-link and electric fencing is used at East Lake colonies at the Lower Rio Grande Valley NWR in Texas to exclude mammalian predators from waterbird nesting areas (D. S. Stolley, pers. comm.). Electric fencing is also used at Sonny Bono Salton Sea NWR to exclude predators, primarily raccoons.

Artificial Nesting Habitat

In 2005, at the Sonny Bono Salton Sea NWR, the USFWS experimented with a small floating raft in a freshwater impoundment to augment existing nesting habitat (C. C. Schoneman, pers. comm.). Gull-billed Tern decoys and a sound system to broadcast recorded Gull-billed Tern colony vocalizations were placed on the raft. No Gull-billed Terns nested on the raft in 2005 but at least five pairs nested on the raft in 2006, although no nests successfully hatched (C. C. Schoneman, pers. comm.). Gull-billed Tern fledglings and parents also used the raft late in the season for loafing and roosting. Successful nesting by Gull-billed Terns occurred in 2007 with approximately 30 nests established on the raft (KCM). In 2006, a second and larger nesting platform, also using decoys and recordings, was constructed on stilts in the Salton Sea (M. A. Ricca, pers. comm.). This platform was not used by Gull-billed Terns but was colonized by four pairs of nesting Black Skimmers. In 2007, a maximum of 28 Gull-billed Tern nests were observed on the platform, with minimal nest and fledgling success (KCM). Ramps were installed on the raft and elevated platforms to assist chicks to nest sites if they fell from or left the site before fully fledging off. Strong winds and waves damaged the integrity of ramps at both sites, requiring modification and annual maintenance (C. C. Schoneman, pers. comm.). Although the value of artificial nesting platforms is unclear, their potential benefit of providing nesting habitat free from human disturbance and mammalian predators merits further study (C. C. Schoneman, pers. comm.).

Education

Apart from signs at various colony sites and interpretive information provided at some federal and state wildlife refuges, there is little or no outreach specifically relating to Gull-billed Terns. On the east coast, the Virginia Coastal Bird Partnership, a program involving agencies, research institutions, and conservation organizations, was formed in 1993 to monitor waterbirds and educate the public about them; Gull-billed Terns have been a specific focus of this group (RME). In southern California, Gull-billed Terns have received a negative public perception because of their observed predation on two species listed under the ESA (KCM). Discussions with managers of the listed species' habitats are needed to develop management actions benefiting all three species.

Conservation Recommendations

Our recommendations for range-wide conservation practices for both *G. n. aranea* and *G. n. vanrossemi* emphasize monitoring, habitat management and protection, and research. These recommendations are in priority order within each section.

Monitoring

(1) Conduct breeding population surveys focused specifically on Gull-billed Terns. Small colony size and unique nest sites, substrates, and seasonality may cause colonies to be overlooked during multi-species surveys and aerial waterbird surveys may fail to distinguish Gull-billed Tern nests from those of other terns.

(a) Standardize survey methodology recognizing that it may need to be modified for location, size, distribution, and habitat of an individual colony.

(b) Report abundance in number of pairs whenever possible, so that data are comparable across regions. Measure "number of adults" rather than "number of nest attempts" given the species' low nest site tenacity and re-nesting ability.

(c) Coordinate the seasonal timing of Gull-billed Tern surveys within regions.

(d) Conduct range-wide surveys every three to five years as Gull-billed Tern populations may fluctuate inter-annually and site fidelity is relatively low. More frequent surveys (i.e., annually) for the subspecies *G. n. vanrossemi* are recommended.

(e) On state, federal, and other managed conservation lands, survey Gull-billed Tern colony sites annually for presence (or absence) of nesting birds. If the colony consists only of Gull-billed Terns, conduct a single survey to coincide with the peak incubation period. If other species are present, conduct a visit timed specifically for Gull-billed Terns.

(f) Conduct baseline surveys along the Gulf of Mexico Coast in Mexico to determine breeding distribution, colony status, and abundance of *G. n. aranea*. Once this has been determined, conduct periodic surveys as described in (d), above.

(2) Minimize disturbance to nesting colonies by conducting surveys outside the colony, wherever possible, using observers in blinds or vehicles or observing from a distance to prevent flushing.

(3) Count fledging and near-fledging age young approximately three weeks after the first chick has hatched on the colony to measure breeding success.

(4) Explore the potential for conducting surveys of Gull-billed Terns in the species' winter range from the Gulf of Mexico coast states south through Mexico, Central America, the Caribbean, and northern South America to determine winter distribution and the overlap in wintering by both *G. n. aranea* and *G. n. vanrossemi* and to aid in determining conservation needs on the wintering grounds.

(5) Use field identification cards of Gull-billed Terns to train surveyors to identify both breeding and wintering terns and to estimate the approximate age of pre-fledged young.

Habitat Management and Protection

Protection of nesting and foraging habitat of Gull-billed Terns is vital to the long-term survival of the species. Conservation programs aimed at reducing or reversing the impacts of river channelization, changes in sediment deposition, beach erosion, sea level increases, regional water transfers, and other landscape level perturbations will ensure the long-term viability of Gull-billed Tern habitat. Because most Gull-billed Terns spend their annual cycle in the United States and either Mexico, Central America, or the Caribbean, conservation efforts will require multi-national cooperation. Laws protecting habitat range-wide and prohibiting take in countries outside the United States require better enforcement. Increased international communication and cooperation between biologists may help refine conservation strategies.

(1) Evaluate active and historic colony sites to identify opportunities to enhance or protect colonies. Develop and implement colony specific management plans to improve colony security and reproductive success and to reduce threats.

(a) Reduce erosion of nesting islands by supplementing with crushed shell, gravel, or sand (0.2-0.4 mm) and/or installing riprap borders where necessary and feasible.

(b) Manage vegetation growth to heights of less than 12 cm and densities of less than 14% cover, as indicated by Parnell et al. (1995), to provide suitable open space for Gull-billed Tern colonies.

(c) Assess active colonies to determine the need for predator management Design and implement an integrated predator management program using non-lethal (e.g., fencing) and, where necessary, lethal predator control measures in coordination with state and federal agencies. Implement measures to control feral and domestic pets that impact colony nesting success.

(2) Seek long-term protection for all colony sites through land acquisition or conservation easements or agreements.

(3) Seek long-term protection of upland foraging habitats through land acquisition or conservation easements or agreements.

(4) In coordination with ESA recovery teams, design and implement a multi-species management strategy for Gull-billed and California Least terns, western Snowy Plovers, and other ground-nesting waterbirds in coastal southern California.

(5) Given the importance of the Salton Sea to *G. n. vanrossemi*, ensure that restoration and management plans for the Salton Sea address the subspecies' long-term habitat needs.

(6) Reduce or limit lethal control of Gull-billed Terns at aquaculture farms in northwestern Mexico.

(7) Provide informational signs and other outreach material at colony sites to reduce human disturbance.

Research

(1) Develop standardized monitoring and analytical protocol for trend analysis in range-wide surveys.

(2) Investigate the subspecies taxonomy of Gull-billed Terns.

(3) Develop techniques to identify and establish alternative nesting sites in southern California for *G. n. vanrossemi* to decrease conflicts with California Least Terns and western Snowy Plovers.

(4) Use video monitoring techniques at co-occurring *G. n. vanrossemi*, California Least Tern, and western Snowy Plover nests to evaluate the impacts of Gull-billed Tern predation.

(5) Develop population viability models for Gull-billed and California Least terns and western Snowy Plovers to assess each species' population health and to evaluate the effects of Gull-billed Tern predation.

(6) Conduct long-term studies to determine age and sex-specific mortality, fecundity rates, and lifetime reproductive success for both subspecies.

(7) Investigate specific foraging patterns of Gull-billed Tern adults.

(8) Investigate winter distribution and ecology of colonies breeding in the United States and Mexico through banding, auxiliary marking, and telemetry.

(9) In conjunction with surveys in Mexico and Central America, take measurements and collect specimens or tissues of breeding birds to delineate the southern limits of the breeding ranges of both *G. n. aranea* and *G. n. vanrossemi* and to determine the subspecific identity of breeding birds in Central America.

(10) Investigate contaminants in Gull-billed Terns that may result from foraging in agricultural areas.

(11) Investigate the value of artificial nesting platforms.

(12) Determine nest success of roof-nesting Gull-billed Tern populations to determine the importance of this substrate to breeding populations.

(13) Gather information on lethal control of *G. n. vanrossemi* at shrimp farms in western Mexico to determine effects to the subspecies' population.

Conclusion

The current population of the subspecies *G. n. aranea* in the United States is estimated to be approximately 3610 pairs, with over 60% occurring in Texas. This species is possibly extirpated in Maryland and Delaware. The number of pairs has declined in Virginia, North Carolina, Florida, and possibly Georgia, but appears stable in Texas. The subspecies *G. n. vanrossemi* has 737 to 808 breeding pairs in western Mexico and California. Trend information for *G. n. vanrossemi* is unavailable because of the lack of data from Mexico prior to 2003. The main causes of population declines in North America are disturbance of nesting colonies, loss of natural nesting islands, and development or modification of upland foraging habitats.

Literature Cited

Alvarez-Borrego, S. 2001. The Colorado River estuary and upper Gulf of California, Baja, Mexico. Pages 331–340 *in* U. Seeliger and B. Kjerfve, editors. Coastal Marine Ecosystems of Latin America. Ecological Studies, Vol. 144. Springer-Verlag, Berlin, Germany.

Bent, A. C. 1921. Life histories of North American gulls and terns. U.S. National Museum Bulletin 113, Washington, D.C.

Blake, E. R. 1977. Manual of neotropical birds, Vol. 1. University of Chicago Press, Chicago, Illinois.

Blus, L. J. 1984. DDE in bird's eggs: comparison of two methods for estimating critical levels. Wilson Bulletin 96:268-276.

Blus, L. J., and C. J. Stafford. 1980. Breeding biology and relation of pollutants to Black Skimmers and Gull-billed Terns in South Carolina. Special Scientific Report-Wildlife No. 230, U.S. Fish and Wildlife Service, Washington, D.C.

Brinker, D. F. 1996. Gull-billed Tern. Pages 160-161 *in* C.S. Robbins and E. A. T. Blom, editors. Atlas of the breeding birds of Maryland and the District of Columbia. University of Pittsburgh Press, Pittsburgh, Pennsylvania.

Brinker, D. F., J. M. McCann, B. Williams, and B. D. Watts. 2007. Colonial nesting seabirds in the Chesapeake region: where have we been and where are we going? Pages 93-104 *in* R. M. Erwin, B. D. Watts, G. M. Haramis, M. C. Perry, and K. A. Hobson, editors. Waterbirds of the Chesapeake Bay and vicinity: harbingers of change? Waterbirds Special Publication 1.

Brinker, D. F., J. M. McCann, B. Williams, and B. D. Watts. 2008. Colonial nesting seabirds in the Chesapeake region: where have we been and where are we going? (Errata). Waterbirds 31:670.

Buckley, P. A., and F. G. Buckley. 1984. Seabirds of the North and Middle Atlantic coast of the United States: their status and conservation. Pages 101–133 *in* J. Croxall, P. G. H. Evans, and R. W. Schreiber, editors. Status and conservation of the worlds' seabirds. International Council for Bird Preservation, Technical Publication No. 2, Paston Press, Norwich, England.

Bull, J. 1964. Birds of the New York area. Harper and Row, New York City, New York.

Burger, J., and M. Gochfeld. 1990. The Black Skimmer: social dynamics of a colonial species. Columbia University Press, New York City, New York.

Chaney, A. H., B. R. Chapman, K. P. Karges, D. A. Nelson, R. R. Schmidt, and L. C. Thebeau. 1978. Use of dredged material islands by colonial seabirds and wading birds in Texas. Technical Report D-78-8, U.S. Army Engineer Waterways Experiment Station, Vicksburg, Mississippi.

Chardine, J. W., R. D. Morris, J. F. Parnell, and J. Pierce. 2000. Status and conservation priorities for Laughing Gulls, Gull-billed Terns, Royal Terns and Bridled Terns in the West Indies. Pages 65–79 *in* E. A. Schreiber and D. S. Lee, editors. Status and conservation of West Indian Seabirds. Society of Caribbean Ornithology, Special Publication No. 1, Ruston, Louisiana.

Clapp, R. B., and P. A. Buckley. 1984. Status and conservation of seabirds in the southeastern United States. Pages 135–155 *in* J. Croxall, P. G. H. Evans, and R. W. Schreiber, editors. Status and conservation of the worlds' seabirds. International Council for Bird Preservation, Technical Publication, No. 2, Paston Press, Norwich, England.

Clapp, R. B., P. A. Buckley, and F. G. Buckley. 1993. Conservation of temperate North Pacific terns. Pages 154–163 *in* K. Vermeer, K. T. Briggs, K. H. Morgan, and D. Siegel-Causey, editors. The status, ecology, and conservation of marine birds of the North Pacific. Canadian Wildlife Service Special Publication, Ottawa, Ontario.

Clapp, R. B., M. K. Klimkiewicz, and J. H. Kennard. 1982. Longevity records of North American birds: Gaviidae through Alcidae. Journal of Field Ornithology 53:81-208.

Clapp, R. B., D. Morgan-Jacobs, and R. C. Banks. 1983. Marine birds of the southeastern United States and Gulf of Mexico. Part 3: Charadriiformes. FWS/OBS-83/30, U.S. Fish and Wildlife Service, Division of Biological Services, Washington, D.C.

Clement, R. C. 1946. Some Louisiana observations. Auk 63:97-99.

Coburn, L. M. 1996. Gull-billed tern nesting on a roof in northwest Florida. Florida Field Naturalist 24:76-77.

Contreras-Balderas, A. J. 1993. Avifauna de Laguna Madre, Tamaulipas. Pages 553-558 *in* S. I. Salazar-Vallejo y N. E. Gonzalez, editors. Biodiversidad Marina y Costera de México. Comisión Nacional de Biodiversidad y Centro de Investigaciónes de Quintana Roo, México.

Correa-Sandoval, J., and J. Garcia-Barron. 1993. Avifauna de Ria Celestun y Ria Lagartos. Pages 641–649 *in* S. I. Salazar-Vallejo y N. E. Gonzalez, editors. Bioversidad Marina y Costera de México. Comisión Nacional Biodiversidad y Centro de Investigaciónes de Quintana Roo, México.

Cramp, S. 1985. Handbook of the birds of Europe, the Middle East, and North Africa, Vol. IV, Terns to Woodpeckers. Oxford University Press, Oxford, England.

Danemann, G. D., and R. Carmona. 2000. Breeding birds of the Guerrero Negro saltworks, Baja California Sur, Mexico. Western Birds 31:195-199.

Densmore, R. J. 1990. Gull-billed Tern predation on a Least Tern chick. Wilson Bulletin 102:180-181.

Dickinson, E. C., editor. 2003. The Howard and Moore complete checklist of the birds of the world. 3rd edition. Princeton University Press, Princeton, New Jersey.

Erickson, R. A., R. A. Hamilton, and S. N. G. Howell. 2001. New information on migrant birds in northern and central portions of the Baja California peninsula, including species new to Mexico. Monographs in Field Ornithology 3:112-170.

Erickson, R. A., R.A. Hamilton, R. Carmona, and E. Palacios. 2004. The nesting season, Baja California Peninsula, North American Birds 58:604-605.

Erickson, R. A., R. A. Hamilton, E. Palacios, and R. Carmona. 2003. The winter season, Baja California Peninsula. North American Birds 57:260-262.

Erwin, R. M. 1979. Coastal waterbird colonies: Cape Elizabeth, Maine to Virginia. FWS/OBS-79/10, U.S. Fish and Wildlife Service, Division of Biological Services, Washington, D.C.

Erwin, R. M., D. H. Allen, and D. Jenkins. 2003. Created versus natural coastal islands: Atlantic waterbird populations, habitat choices, and management implications. Estuaries 26:949-955.

Erwin, R. M., B. R. Truitt, and J. E. Jimenez. 2001. Ground-nesting waterbirds and mammalian carnivores in the Virginia barrier island region: running out of options. Journal of Coastal Research 17:292-296.

Erwin, R. M., T. B. Eyler, J. S. Hatfield, and S. McGary. 1998a. Diets of nestling Gull-billed Terns in coastal Virginia. Colonial Waterbirds 21:323-327.

Erwin, R. M., J. D. Nichols, T. B. Eyler, D. B. Stotts, and B. R. Truitt. 1998b. Modeling colony-site dynamics: a case study of Gull-billed Terns (*Sterna nilotica*) in coastal Virginia. Auk 115:970-978.

Eyler, T. B., R. M. Erwin, D. B. Stotts, and J. S. Hatfield. 1999. Aspects of hatching success and chick survival in Gull-billed Terns in coastal Virginia. Waterbirds 22:54-59.

Gandy, B. E., and W. H. Turcotte. 1970. Catalog of Mississippi bird records. Volume 1. Mississippi Game and Fish Commission, State Wildlife Museum, Jackson, Mississippi.

Garza-Torres, H. A., and A. G. Navarro S. 2003. Breeding records of the Sooty Tern in Tamaulipas and its distribution on the Gulf of Mexico. Huitzil 4:22-25.

Gochfeld, M., and J. Burger. 1996. Family Sternidae (Terns). Pages 624–667 *in* J. del Hoyo, A. Elliott, and J. Sargatal, editors. Handbook of the birds of the world, Vol. 3, Hoatzin to Auks. Lynx Edicions, Barcelona, Spain.

Godfrey, W. E. 1986. The birds of Canada. Revised edition. National Museum of Natural Sciences, Ottawa, Canada.

Gómez de Silva, H. 2007. The winter season. Mexico. North American Birds 61:334-340.

Gonzalez-Bernal, M. A., X. Vega, and E. Mellink. 2003. Nesting of Western Gulls in Bahia de Santa Maria-La Reforma, Sinaloa, Mexico. Western Birds 34:175-176.

Grinnell, J., and A. H. Miller. 1944. The distribution of the birds of California. Pacific Coast Avifauna, No. 27. Cooper Ornithological Club, Berkeley, California.

Hagemeijer, W. J. M., and M. J. Blair, editors. 1997. The European Bird Census Council atlas of European breeding birds. T. and A. D. Poyser Press, London, England.

Hamilton, R. A., and D. R. Willick. 1996. The birds of Orange County, California: status and distribution. Sea and Sage Press, Sea and Sage Audubon Society, Irvine, California.

Higgins, P. J., and S. J. J. F. Davies, editors. 1996. Handbook of Australian, New Zealand and Antarctic birds, Vol. 3. Oxford University Press, Melbourne, Australia.

Howell, S. N. G. 1999. A bird-finding guide to Mexico. Cornell University Press, Ithaca, New York.

Howell, S. N. G., and S. Webb. 1995. A guide to the birds of Mexico and northern Central America. Oxford University Press, Oxford, England.

Instituto Technologico de Sonora. 2004. Hidrogeomorfología y ecología de los humedales costeros del Norte de Sinaloa y el Sur de Sonora: criterios para inventariar, valorar, ordenar, y conservar los ecosistemas costeros del Noroeste de México. Departamento del Ciencias del Agua y del Medioambiente. <www.itson.mx/drn/dcama> (5 April 2006)

Jones, H. L. 2003. Birds of Belize. University of Texas Press, Austin, Texas.

Kress, S. W., E. H. Weinstein, and I. C. T. Nisbet. 1983. The status of tern populations in northeastern United States and adjacent Canada. Colonial Waterbirds 6:84-106.

Lehman, P. E. 1994. The birds of Santa Barbara County, California. Vertebrate Museum, University of California, Santa Barbara, California.

Martin, R. P., and G. D. Lester. 1990. Atlas and census of wading bird and seabird nesting colonies in Louisiana, 1990. Louisiana Department of Wildlife and Fisheries, Louisiana Natural Heritage Program, Special Publication No. 3, Baton Rouge, Louisiana.

McCaskie, G. 1976. The nesting season, southern Pacific Coast. American Birds 30:1004.

McCaskie G. 1986. The nesting season, southern Pacific Coast. American Birds 40:1255.

McCaskie, G., and K. L. Garrett. 2001. The spring migration, southern Pacific Coast. North American Birds 55:356.

McCaskie, G., and K. L. Garrett. 2004. The nesting season, southern Pacific Coast. North American Birds 57:545.

McCaskie, G., and K. L. Garrett. 2005. Fall migration, southern Pacific Coast. North American Birds 59:149.

McWilliams, G. M., and D. W. Brauning. 2000. The birds of Pennsylvania. Cornell University Press, Ithaca, New York.

Michot, T.C., C. W. Jeske, W. J. Vermillion, J. Mazourek, and S. Kemmerer. 2004. Atlas and census of wading bird and seabird nesting colonies in south Louisiana, 2001. Baratara Terrebonne National Estuary Program Report No. 32. Thibodaux, Louisiana.

Molina, K. C. 2004. Breeding larids of the Salton Sea: trends in population size and colony site occupation. Studies in Avian Biology 27:92-99.

Molina, K. C., and R. M. Erwin. 2006. The distribution and conservation status of the Gull-billed Tern (*Gelochelidon nilotica*) in North America. Waterbirds 29:271-295.

Molina, K. C., and K. L. Garrett. 2001. The breeding birds of Cerro Prieto geothermal ponds, Mexicali Valley, Baja California. Monographs in Field Ornithology 3:23-28.

Molina, K. C., and D. A. Marschalek. 2003. Foraging behavior and diet of breeding Western Gull-billed Terns (*Sterna nilotica vanrossemi*) in San Diego Bay, California. California Department of Fish and Game, Habitat Conservation and Recovery Program, 2003-01, Sacramento, California.

Molina, K. C., K. L. Garrett, K. W. Larson, and D. P. Craig. 2009. The winter distribution of the western Gull-billed Tern (*Gelochelidon nilotica vanrossemi*). Western Birds 40:2-20.

Moller, A. P. 1975. Ynglebstanden af Sandterne (*Gelochelidon nilotica nilotica* Gmel.) i 1972 i Europa, Afrika og det vestlige Asien med en oversight over bestandsaendringer i dette arhundrede. Dansk Ornithologisk Forenings Tidsskrift 69:1-8.

Monroe, B. L., Jr. 1968. A distributional survey of the birds of Honduras. Ornithological Monographs 7.

Monson, G., and A. R. Phillips. 1981. Annotated checklist of the birds of Arizona. University of Arizona Press, Tucson, Arizona.

NatureServe Explorer. 2006. NatureServe Explorer: an online encyclopedia of life <www.natureserve.org/explorer> (7 September 2009).

O'Connell, T. J., and R. A. Beck. 2003. Gull predation limits nesting success of terns and skimmers on the Virginia barrier islands. Journal of Field Ornithology 74:66-73.

Páez-Osuna, F., A. Gracia-Gasca, F. Flores-Verdugo, L. P. Lyle-Fritch, R. Alonso-Rodríguez, A. Roque, and A. C. Ruiz-Fernández. 2003. Shrimp aquaculture development and the environment in the Gulf of California ecoregion. Marine Pollution Bulletin 46:806-815.

Palacios, E., and E. Mellink. 2007. The colonies of VanRossem's Gull-billed Tern (*Gelochelidon nilotica vanrossemi*) in Mexico. Waterbirds 30:214-222.

Parnell, J. R., and R. F. Soots, Jr. 1979. Atlas of colonial waterbirds of North Carolina estuaries. UNC-SG-78-10, North Carolina State University, UNC Sea Grant, Raleigh, North Carolina.

Parnell, J. F., R. M. Erwin, and K. C. Molina. 1995. Gull-billed Tern (*Sterna nilotica*). *In* A. Poole and F. Gill, editors. The Birds of North America, No. 140. Academy of Natural Sciences, Philadelphia, Pennsylvania; American Ornithologists' Union, Washington, D.C.

Parnell, J. R., W. W. Golder, M. A. Shields, T. L. Quay, and T. M. Henson. 1997. Changes in nesting populations of colonial waterbirds in coastal North Carolina 1900–1995. Colonial Waterbirds 20:458-469.

Patten, M. A., G. McCaskie, and P. Unitt. 2003. Birds of the Salton Sea: status, biogeography, and ecology. University of California Press, Berkeley, California.

Pemberton, J. R. 1922. A large tern colony in Texas. Condor 24:37-48.

Pemberton, J.R. 1927. The American Gull-billed Tern breeding in California. Condor 29:253-258.

Peresbarbosa, E., and E. Mellink. 2001. Nesting waterbirds of Isla Montague, northern Gulf of California, Mexico: loss of eggs due to predation and flooding, 1993–1994. Waterbirds 24:265-271.

Pius, S. M., and P. L. Leberg. 1997. Aggression and nest spacing in single and mixed species groups of seabirds. Oecologia 111:144-150.

Pius, S. M., and P. L. Leberg. 1998. The protector species hypothesis: do Black Skimmers find refuge from predators in Gull-billed Tern colonies? Ethology 104:273-284.

Pius, S. M., and P. L. Leberg. 2002. Experimental assessment of the influence of Gull-billed Terns on nest site choice of Black Skimmers. Condor 104:174-177.

Portnoy, J. W. 1977. Nesting colonies of seabirds and wading birds: coastal Louisiana, Mississippi, and Alabama. FWS/OBS-7707, U.S. Fish and Wildlife Service, Division of Biological Services, Washington, D.C.

Portnoy, J. W., R. M. Erwin, and T. W. Custer. 1981. Atlas of gull and tern colonies: North Carolina to Key West, Florida (including pelicans, cormorants, and skimmers). FWS/OBS-80/05, U.S. Fish and Wildlife Service, Division of Biological Services, Washington, D.C.

Price, J., S. Droege, and A. Price. 1995. The summer atlas of North American birds. Academic Press, San Diego, California.

Purrington, R. D. 2002. The nesting season, central southern region. North American Birds 56:447.

Quinn, J. S., and D. A. Wiggins. 1990. Differences in prey delivered to chicks by individual Gull-billed Terns. Colonial Waterbirds 13:67-69.

Rangel-Salazar, J. L., P. L. Enriquez-Rocha, and J. Guzman-Poo. 1993. Colonias de reproducción de aves costeras en Sian Ka'an. Pages 833–840 *in* S. I. Salazar-Vallejo y N. E. Gonzalez, editors. Bioversidad Marina y Costera de México. Comisión Nacional Biodiversidad y Centro de Investigaciones de Quintana Roo, México.

Remsen, J. V., Jr. 1978. Bird species of special concern in California. Nongame Wildlife Investigations, Wildlife Management Branch Administrative Report 78-1. California Department of Fish and Game, Sacramento, California.

Ridgely, R. S., and P. J. Greenfield. 2001. The birds of Ecuador: status, distribution and taxonomy. Cornell University Press, Ithaca, New York.

Ridgely, R. S., and J. A. Gwynne, Jr. 1989. A guide to the birds of Panama. 2nd edition. Princeton University Press, Princeton, New Jersey.

Rydzewski, W. 1978. The longevity of ringed birds. Ring 96-97:218-262

Sauer, J. R., J. E. Hines, and J. Fallon. 2008. The North American breeding bird survey, results and analysis 1966–2007. Version 5.15. U.S. Department of Interior, Geological Survey, Patuxent Wildlife Research Center, Laurel, Maryland. <www.mbr-pwrc.usgs.gov/bbs/> (25 August 2009).

Sears, H. F. 1978. Nesting behavior of the Gull-billed Tern. Bird-Banding 49:1-16

Sears, H. F. 1979. Colonial nesting as an anti-predator adaptation in the Gull-billed Tern. Auk 96:202-203.

Secretaría de Medio Ambiente y Recursos Naturales (SEMARNAT). 2002. Norma Oficial Mexicana NOM-059-ECOL-2001. Protección ambiental—Especies nativas de México de flora y fauna silvestres—categoría de riesgo y especificaciones para su inclusión, exclusión o cambio—lista de especies de riesgo. Diario Oficial de la Federación, Órgano del Gobierno Constitucional de Estados Unidos Mexicanos. Marzo 6 de 2002. Tomo DLXXXII N° 4:1-80.

Skorupa, J.P. and H.M. Ohlendorf. 1991. Contaminants in drainage water and avian risk thresholds. Pages 345–368 *in* A. Dinar and D. Zilberman, editors. The Economics and Management of Water and Drainage in Agriculture. Kluwer Academic Publishers. Norwell, Massachusetts.

Sibley, D. A. 2000. The Sibley guide to birds. Alfred A. Knopf, Inc., New York City, New York.

Smith, H. T., and E. M. Alvear. 1997. Recent breeding reports of the Gull-billed Tern in Florida: status undetermined. Florida Naturalist 70:22-23.

Smith, H. T., and J. A. Gore. 1996. Gull-billed Tern. Pages 624-632 *in* J. A. Rodgers, Jr., H. W. Kale, and H. T. Smith, editors. Rare and Endangered Biota of Florida, Vol. V: Birds. University Press of Florida, Gainesville, Florida.

Spendelow, J. A., and S. R. Patton. 1988. National atlas of coastal waterbird colonies in the contiguous United States: 1976–1982. U.S. Fish and Wildlife Service Biological Report 88(5), Washington, D.C.

Stiles, F. G., and A. F. Skutch. 1989. A guide to the birds of Costa Rica. Cornell University Press, Ithaca, New York.

Urban, E. K., C. H. Fry, and S. Keith. 1986. The birds of Africa. Volume 2. Academic Press, London, England.

U.S. Fish and Wildlife Service. 2004. Texas Coastal Program. U.S. Department of Interior, Fish and Wildlife Service. <www.fws.gov/ texascoastalprogram> (25 August 2009).

U.S. Fish and Wildlife Service. 2008. Birds of conservation concern-2008. U.S. Department of Interior, Fish and Wildlife Service, Division of Migratory Bird Management, Administrative Report, Arlington, Virginia. <www.fws.gov/ migratorybirds/NewReportsPublications/ SpecialTopics/BCC2008/BCC2008.pdf> (25 August 2009).

Veit, R. R., and W. R. Petersen. 1993. Birds of Massachusetts. Natural History of New England Series, Massachusetts Audubon Society, Lincoln, Massachusetts.

Walsh, J., V. Elia, R. Kane, and T. Halliwell. 1999. Birds of New Jersey. New Jersey Audubon Society, Bernardsville, New Jersey.

Wells, D. R. 1999. The Birds of the Thai-Malay Peninsula, Vol. 1. Academic Press, San Diego, California.

Wilbur, S. R. 1987. Birds of Baja California. University of California Press, Berkeley, California.

Wittenberger, J. F., and G. L. Hunt, Jr. 1985. The adaptive significance of coloniality in birds. Pages 2–78 *in* D. S. Farner, J. R. King, and K. C. Parkes, editors. Avian Biology, Vol. 8. Academic Press, Orlando, Florida.

Appendix A: State and Regional Summaries of *Gelochilidon nilotica aranea* Status Within the Breeding Range in the U.S., Mexico, and Caribbean[a]

UNITED STATES

Alabama

Summary: Imhof (1976) considered Gull-billed Terns uncommon summer residents, with breeding restricted to islands in the southwestern part of the state, in Mobile Bay and the Mississippi Sound in Mobile County. They occur more commonly as migrants on Alabama's Gulf of Mexico Coast (> 75 birds observed on 6 Aug 1960) with small numbers wintering in upper Mobile Bay and the Mississippi Sound (Imhof 1976). In recent years, small colonies of Gull-billed Terns (totaling only a few dozen breeding pairs) have been found on Gaillard Island, a dredged material island in Mobile Bay, and on two natural barrier islands, Dauphin and Pelican islands, in the Mississippi Sound (Fig. A-1).

Population Trends: Breeding Gull-billed Terns were apparently never abundant in Alabama during the 1900s. Small numbers of Gull-billed Terns were first documented from Petit Bois Island, near the Mississippi/Alabama border, on 4 July 1913, where only about 15 or 20 pairs were believed to be nesting (Howell 1924). Three active nests were reported at Cedar Point in 1956 (Imhoff 1976) and 23 individuals were reported on Dauphin Island in 1976 (Portnoy 1977). More recently, as many as 87 pairs have nested in Alabama (Table A-1; R. B. Clay, pers. comm.). Although breeding numbers are highly variable, an average of about 50 pairs nested annually at one to three colonies from 1988–2004 (Fig. A-1; Tables 2, A-1).

Research/Monitoring: Research focused on Gull-billed Terns has not been conducted in Alabama. Comprehensive surveys were conducted in the state in 1976 and 1983. Since 2001, state-wide censuses have been conducted annually (R. B. Clay, pers. comm.). Field work for a state Breeding Bird Atlas is currently underway (R. B. Clay pers. comm.).

Conservation/Management Activities: Dauphin and Pelican islands are privately owned, while Gaillard Island is an active dredge disposal site owned by the state. No conservation or management activities specific to nesting waterbirds occur at these sites (R. B. Clay, pers. comm.).

State Status: Protected (Alabama Natural Heritage Program 2008).

Natural Heritage Rank: S2—Imperiled (NatureServe Explorer 2006).

Habitat Conditions: In Alabama, nesting occurs on undeveloped, low elevation sandy shoal islands sparsely vegetated with dune grasses and on a dredged-material island that provides bare nesting substrate (R. B. Clay, pers. comm.).

Threats: All three islands are of low relief and breeding efforts may be swamped by the surge of early season tropical storms and hurricanes (R. B. Clay, pers. comm.). Human disturbance can be significant on Dauphin and Pelican islands (R. B. Clay, pers. comm.).

[a] See Appendix C for contact information for contributors to the state and regional summaries.

Table A-1. Number of Gull-billed Tern breeding pairs at colonies in Mobile County, Alabama, 1988–2004 (R. B. Clay, pers. comm.). Dash (—) indicates data are insufficient to discern site availability, occupancy, or extent of survey coverage for a particular site and year.

Colony	1988	1989	1990	1991	1992	1993	1994	1995	1996	1997	1998	1999	2000	2001	2002	2003	2004
Dauphin I. (west end)	—	—	—	—	—	—	—	—	—	—	—	—	—	15	0	0	30
Gaillard I.	59	57	72	3	34	90	12	58	39	14	75	10	2	5	0	9	20
Pelican I.	—	—	—	—	—	—	—	—	—	—	—	35	50	67	50	0	35
Totals	59	57	72	3	34	90	12	58	39	14	75	45	52	87	50	9	70

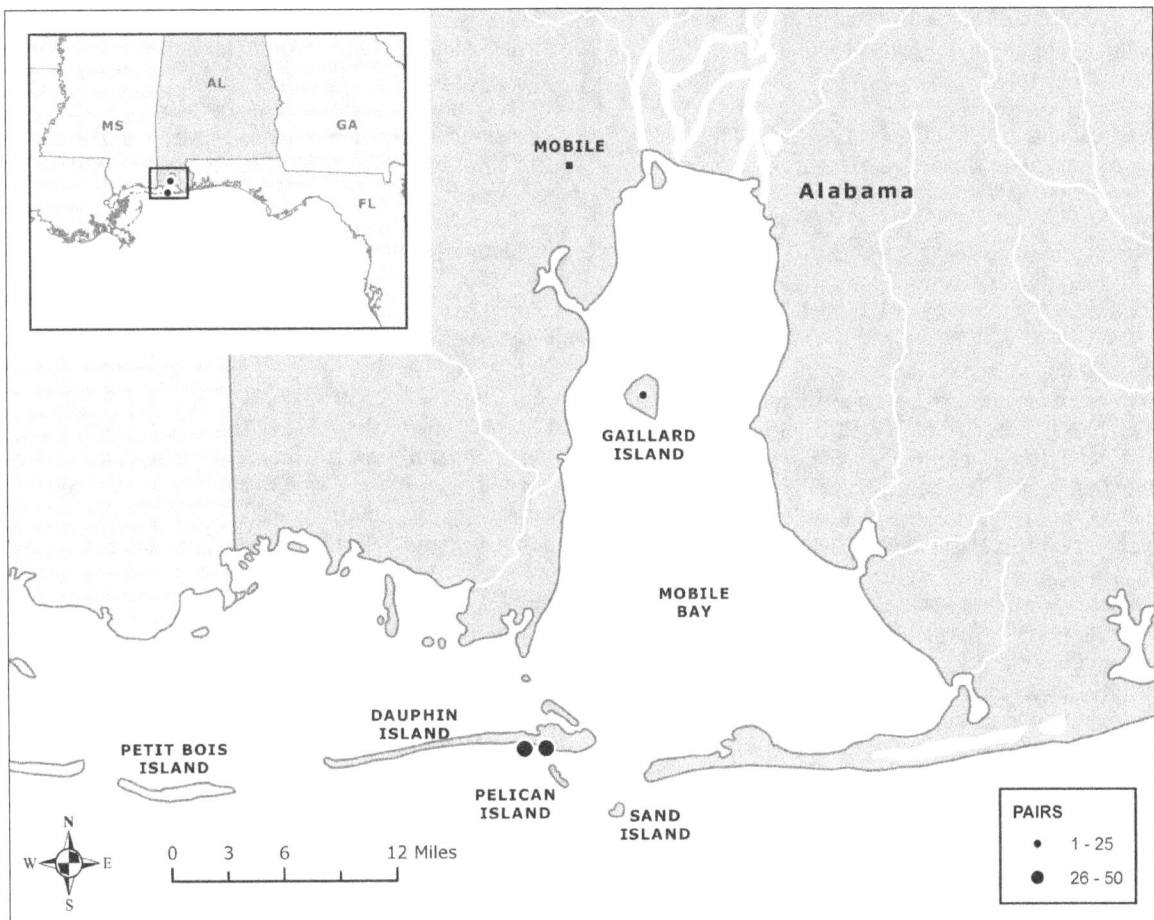

Figure A-1. Locations and sizes of Gull-billed Tern colonies in Alabama, 2004.

Delaware and Maryland

Summary: Gull-billed Terns have bred sporadically and in very small numbers in at least two known sites in Delaware. At Rehobeth Bay and Assawoman Wildlife Refuge, between 1958 and 1991 (Hess et al. 2000). Gull-billed Terns are virtually extirpated in Maryland and are considered rare summer residents with records primarily from Worcester County in the extreme southeastern portion of the state. The species has nested at South Point dredged-material islands, Clam Harbor Tumps, Oyster Island, Big Bay Marsh, and Ocean City spoil, all in Worcester County (Brinker 1996). The numbers of breeding pairs in Maryland peaked in the 1950s and 1960s, and since 1986, the state has seen intermittent breeding by only a single pair. Unsuitability of sand and shell dredged-material due to island erosion or vegetation succession has been a factor in the virtual extirpation of this species from Maryland.

Population Trends: Breeding in Delaware was first documented in 1958, when three clutches were collected at Rehobeth Bay (Hess et al. 2000). Gull-billed Terns possibly bred at Assawoman Wildlife Area in 1958; breeding was documented there in 1959 and in 1989–1991. No breeding was documented from 1983–1987 and there has been no documented nesting since 1991 (Hess et al. 2000).

Gull-billed Terns were never numerous historically in Maryland (Brinker 1996). The species colonized the South Point dredged-material islands in 1945 and continued to breed there until the early 1960s. During the 1950s, 25 to 30 pairs were recorded but the number of breeding pairs was considerably lower than that in most years. During the 1970s, the maximum number of breeding pairs was three and the species ceased to breed in the state from 1977–1983. From 1985–1988, nine, 33, one, and zero pairs nested, respectively, and were limited to a single site in any one year (Brinker 1996). The location of the last confirmed breeding was Big Bay Marsh, where possibly one pair has bred intermittently from 2000–2004 (D. F. Brinker, pers. comm.).

Research /Monitoring: Breeding Bird Atlas field work was conducted from 1983–1987 in Delaware (Hess et al. 2000) and Maryland (Brinker 1996). Census and monitoring efforts in Delaware are unknown but are conducted irregularly in Maryland.

Conservation /Management Activities: No active conservation or management measures are currently conducted.

State Status: None in Delaware; Endangered in Maryland (Maryland Department of Natural Resources 2007).

Natural Heritage Rank: SHB, S2N—Possibly extirpated in Delaware; S1—Critically Imperiled in Maryland (NatureServe Explorer 2006).

Habitat Conditions: In Delaware, breeding habitat consisted of salt marshes from Indian River Inlet north to Bombay Hook NWR. In Maryland, nesting was on dredged-material islands in barren areas of sand and shell. The South Point dredged-material islands in Maryland became unsuitable due to vegetation succession by the early 1960s, and Clam Harbor Tumps and Oyster Island have eroded to below mean sea level (Brinker 1996). Big Bay Marsh, Maryland, is a narrow (2–3 m) shell beach of such low elevation that it hardly extends above wind-driven storm tides. In Maryland, Gull-billed Terns foraged in open salt marshes, fields and along beaches (Brinker 1996).

Threats: None described in Delaware. In Maryland, succession of vegetation on some dredged-material islands is believed to render them unsuitable for nesting (Brinker 1996). The limited number of available nesting sites in reasonable proximity to feeding areas and the loss of two previously used nesting islands due to erosion are believed to have contributed to their apparent extirpation from the state (Brinker 1996).

Florida

Summary: Florida's Breeding Bird Atlas (Florida Fish and Wildlife Commission 2003) considers Gull-billed Terns to be rare and highly localized breeders in the state. Breeding populations in Duval and Brevard counties totaled several hundred pairs in the mid-1970s, but overall numbers of birds as well as occupied colony sites have since declined, likely a result of modification and degradation of coastal habitats. The first Florida nest was recorded in 1932 at Pensacola in Escambia County (Weston 1933); however, an egg set collected in 1892 from Anna Maria Island in Manatee County predates the Pensacola nest. Except for a colony in the interior of Palm Beach County and on islands in Lake Okeechobee, nesting by Gull-billed Terns has been restricted to the northern half of the state. Gull-billed Terns have nested in Duval and Brevard counties on the Atlantic Coast, in Bay and Franklin counties in the Panhandle, in the Tampa Bay area in Pinellas and Hillsborough counties (Florida Fish and Wildlife Conservation Commission 2003), and inland, at the phosphate mines of Polk and Hillsborough counties (Smith and Gore 1996).

Presently, most nesting occurs in the St. John's River estuary in Duval County and in Tampa Bay (Fig. A-2). Most Gull-billed Terns depart Florida for the winter, but small numbers remain on the Atlantic coast north to Jacksonville and on the Gulf coast north to the Tampa Bay area (Stevenson and Anderson 1994).

Population Trends: No comprehensive survey data are available for the state but a strong downward trend is evident. Ogden (1975) reported a total of 534 pairs nesting near Merritt Island in Brevard County and the St. John's River estuary in Duval County in 1975. In 1976 and 1977, census estimates from only one or the other of these two Atlantic coast sites were available, obscuring any indication of trend. Gull-billed Terns were not reported during a study of 40 select dredged-material islands in 1977 (Schreiber and Schreiber 1978). In Franklin County, Smith et al. (1993) reported two to three nests on the St. George Island causeway from 1990–1992. By 2000, populations declined from 1970's levels (to as low as 17 pairs) at the larger Atlantic coast colonies (Merritt and Bird islands, Tables 2, A-2).

Research/Monitoring: No research studies specific to Gull-billed Terns have been conducted. A Breeding Bird Atlas conducted from 1986–1991 confirmed Gull-billed Terns in only 10 of the state's 1028 quadrangles, indicating they are rare and extremely localized breeders in Florida (Florida Fish and Wildlife Conservation Commission 2003). Local coastal censuses were conducted in 1975, 1980–1985, and in 2000. A comprehensive state-wide census for this species has not been undertaken.

Conservation/Management Activities: One of the two largest historic colonies where Gull-billed Terns were known to have nested within Merritt Island NWR and is protected from private development. There is no active management specifically directed at Gull-billed Terns.

State Status: No status

Natural Heritage Rank: S2—Imperiled (NatureServe Explorer 2006).

Habitat Conditions: In Florida, Gull-billed Terns nest on coastal beaches, natural estuarine islands, coastal marshes, dredged-material islands, islands in freshwater lakes, and sand fill at phosphate mining areas. Nesting substrates are sandy and sparsely vegetated. Gull-billed Terns forage in coastal and freshwater marshes, open uplands, shrub-dominated fields, and along coastal beaches (Smith and Gore 1996).

Threats: Loss, modification, and degradation of coastal habitats, including human disturbance, flooding, and succession of vegetation at colony sites are thought to be significant threats to the species (Smith and Gore 1996).

Table A-2. Number of breeding pairs of Gull-billed Terns at colonies in Florida 1973–1977, 1979, 1985, 1995, 1998–2000[a]. Dash (—) indicates data are insufficient to discern site availability, occupancy, or extent of survey coverage for a particular site and year. Data from Clapp et al. 1983, Florida Fish and Wildlife Commission 2003, Loftin and Sutton 1979, Ogden 1974, 1975, 1979, Portnoy et al. 1981, Smith and Alvear 1997.

Colony	1973	1974	1975	1976	1977	1979	1985	1995	1998	1999	2000
Duval Co.											
Bird Islands	—	325	249	121	180	0	0	0	0	0	0
Huguenot Memorial Park	—	—	—	—	—	—	—	25	0	0	10
Mayport Naval Station	—	—	—	—	—	67	0	0	0	0	0
Third Bird Island	—	—	—	—	—	—	—	—	—	2	0
Brevard Co.											
Merritt Island NWR	171	89	285	0	150	0	13	0	0	0	0
Franklin Co.											
Apalachicola, Bird Island	—	—	—	—	—	—	—	—	17	18	6
Hillsborough Co.											
TPA Island 3D	—	—	—	—	—	—	—	—	1	0	1
Totals	171	414	534	121	330	67	13	25	18	20	17

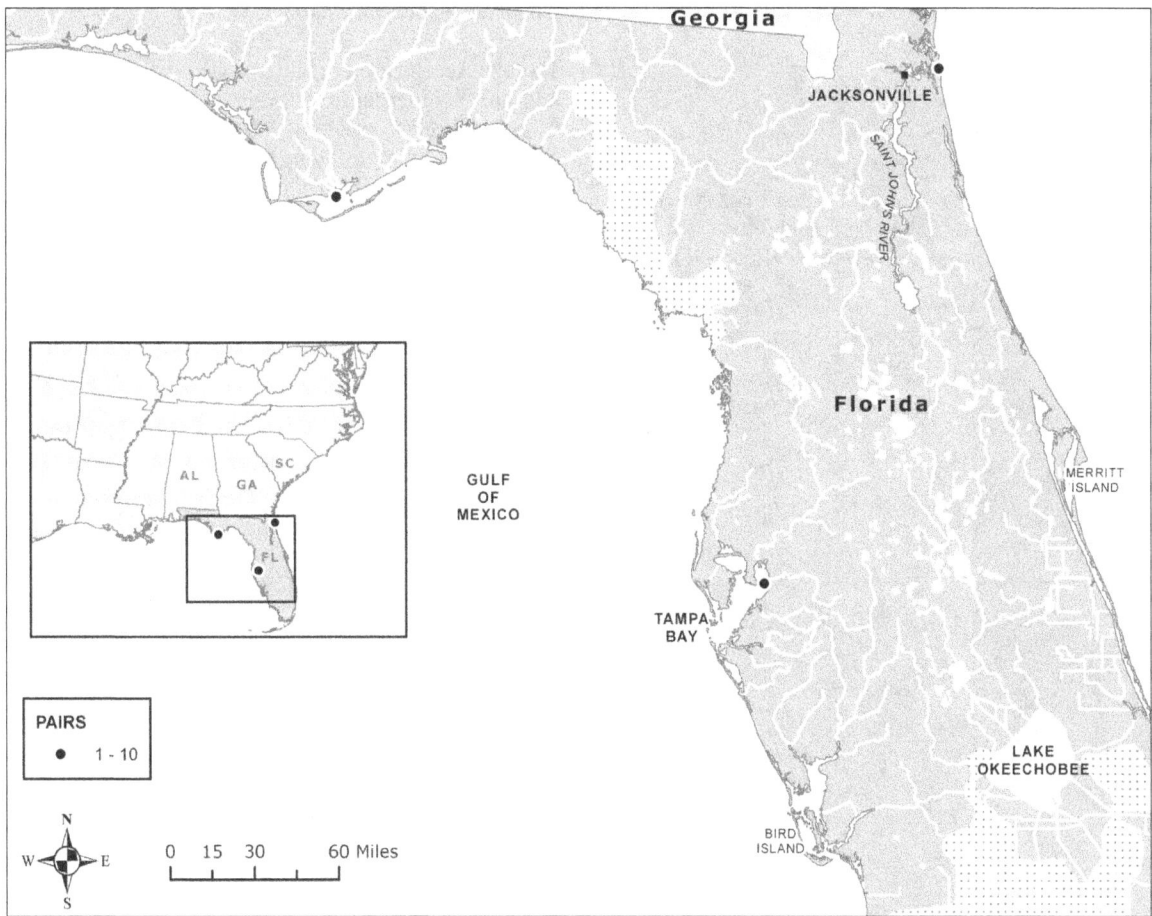

Figure A-2. Locations and sizes of Gull-billed Tern colonies in Florida, 2000.

Georgia

Summary: Breeding populations of Gull-billed Terns in Georgia have historically been small. In recent years only a single island, Little Egg Island Bar, a small, wind-swept and wave-washed sand bar at the mouth of the Altahama River (Kale et al. 1965), has been occupied; about 50 to 100 pairs nest annually on this state-owned island (Clapp et al. 1983). Ericksen (1926) described the first breeding record of four Gull-billed Tern nests on Oysterbed Island in 1926. Gull-billed Terns nested formerly at the mouth of the Savannah River in Chatham County. Burleigh (1958) considered the species to be a scarce summer resident on the coast of Georgia.

Population Trends: Little quantitative data are available for Gull-billed Terns in Georgia prior to the 1990s. During the 1990s, fewer than 100 pairs nested at Little Egg Island Bar (Fig. A-3; Tables 2, A-3). The 2003 census count of 54 pairs at this site may indicate a recent decline (Tables 2, A-3; B. Winn, pers. comm.).

Table A-3. Numbers of breeding pairs of Gull-billed Terns in McIntosh County, Georgia 1993, 1995, 1999 and 2003 (B. Winn, pers. comm.).

Colony	1993	1995	1999	2003
Little Egg Island Bar	65	80	50	54

Research/Monitoring: No research studies specific to Gull-billed Terns have been conducted. Comprehensive surveys were not conducted prior to 1993. Since then waterbird colony censuses have been conducted every two to four years (B. Winn, per. comm.).

Conservation/Management Activities: Only one site, Little Egg Island Bar, is presently active and occurs within a state Protected Natural Area. Management activities at this site include the posting of protective signage to prevent public access year round (B. Winn, pers. comm.). Georgia recently completed its comprehensive plan for the conservation of wildlife and identified the Gull-billed Tern as a high priority species (Georgia Department of Natural Resources 2005).

State Status: Threatened (Georgia Department of Natural Resources 2005).

Natural Heritage Rank: S1—Critically imperiled (NatureServe Explorer 2006).

Habitat Conditions: Given the relatively large tidal fluctuations characteristic of Georgia's coast, the extent of suitable nesting habitat for terns; open and sandy islands, is highly dynamic and often ephemeral in nature (Georgia Department of Natural Resources 2005).

Threats: Accelerated urban growth and development and parallel increases in levels of disturbance by recreationists are believed to be the largest threat to colonial breeding birds in the state (B. Winn, pers. comm.). Predation of eggs and chicks by Laughing Gulls may limit Gull-billed Tern reproductive success (B. Winn, pers. comm.).

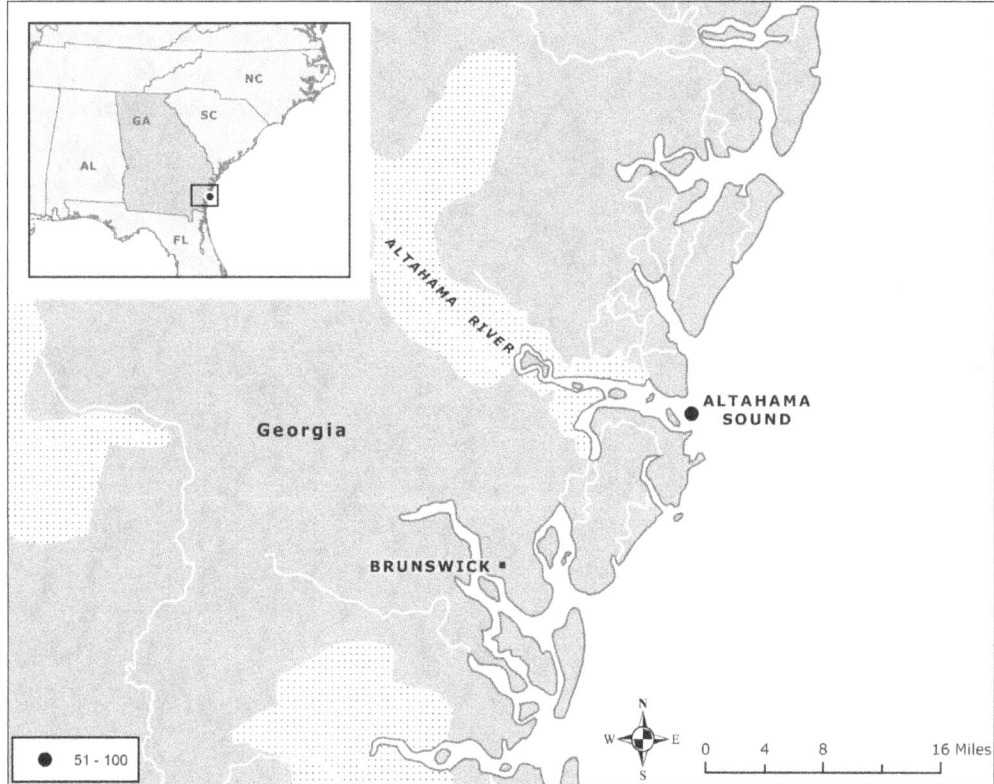

Figure A-3. Locations and sizes of Gull-billed Tern colonies in Georgia, 2003.

Louisiana

Summary: Lowery (1974) considered Gull-billed Terns to be fairly common permanent residents in Louisiana; least numerous in summer, and almost strictly coastal in occurrence. Although Gull-billed Terns are observed in winter in the rice prairie region of Acadia Parish, generally within 30 miles of the coast (W. J. Vermillion, pers. comm.), there is a record farther inland (> 50 miles of the coast) of five individuals over lakes on the Louisiana State University campus in Baton Rouge in September 1965 during Hurricane Betsy (Lowery 1974). Portnoy (1977) considered Gull-billed Terns to be uncommon breeders in Louisiana. The species breeds very locally along the Gulf of Mexico Coast in the Atchafalaya Delta in St. Mary and Terrebonne parishes, and east to islands in Breton and Chandeleur sounds in Plaquemines and St. Bernard parishes. A few Gull-billed Terns are reported to have bred near Sabine Lake at the Louisiana-Texas border (Portnoy 1977) and at Fearman Lake (Martin and Lester 1990). Purrington (2001, 2002) reported recent breeding attempts from the rooftops of several buildings in downtown New Orleans, though success in such colonies is generally low. Most of the recent colonies occur on the central coast, near Marsh Island and Atchafalaya Bay (Fig. A-4; Michot et al. 2004, P. L. Leberg, pers. comm.).

Population Trends: No comprehensive census data are available for the state prior to 1976; however, Louisiana's small Gull-billed Tern population appears to have been relatively stable since the 1990s. Historical records summarized by Portnoy (1977) suggested that Gull-billed Terns had been nesting in very small numbers in the Mississippi River Delta since 1837 and on the western coast since 1906. During the 1960s and early 1970s, up to 11 nests and 27 birds were documented from Grassy Island and the Chandeleur Islands, respectively, in St. Bernard Parish (Portnoy 1977). During the first comprehensive survey of the eastern Gulf of Mexico Coast in 1976, Portnoy (1977) reported 154 pairs (or incubating birds, each assumed to represent an active nest and thus a pair) in four colonies in Louisiana (Table 2), although Clapp et al. (1983) felt Portnoy may have overlooked some nesting areas. Martin and Lester (1990) reported 161 pairs among three colonies during their coastal aerial census in 1990. Results of annual aerial surveys conducted by Linscombe and Vermillion (W. J. Vermillon, pers. comm.) from 1991–1999 ranged from 30 to 1120 incubating adults (Tables 2, A-4). In a survey of dredged-material islands in the Atchafalaya Delta Wildlife Management Area, Leberg et al. (1995) estimated a maximum of 300 to 400 pairs from 1992–1995. Although this survey involved only the central portion of the coast, it is felt to have encompassed most of the known sites. 440 pairs were reported in a 2001 coastal census (Table A-4; T. C. Michot, pers. comm.).

Research/Monitoring: Few studies specifically directed toward Gull-billed Terns have been undertaken in Louisiana. Leberg et al. (1995) examined colony site use by seabirds on dredged-material islands and Mallach and Leberg (1999) examined nest site selection and success among breeding tern and skimmer colonies in the Atchafalaya Delta. Pius and Leberg (1997, 2002) examined aggression and nest spacing in Gull-billed Tern and Black Skimmer colonies and the influence of Gull-billed Terns on nest site choice by Black Skimmers.

Colonial waterbird monitoring in Louisiana has been conducted irregularly in the past. Comprehensive surveys were conducted in 1976, 1978, 1983, 1990, and 1993–1999. Beginning in 2001, comprehensive surveys have been conducted every four years (P. L. Leberg, pers. comm.). Coastal surveys are conducted aerially, either by helicopter or fixed wing aircraft. Rooftop colonies, which may contain up to 100 to 200 pairs (R. D. Purrington, pers. comm.), are generally not included in coastal survey efforts (P. L. Leberg and T. C. Michot, pers. comm.); surveys of these colonies are conducted opportunistically.

Conservation/Management Activities: All recent colony sites occur on state lands and are protected from development.

State Status: Rare Animal of Conservation Concern (Louisiana Department of Wildlife and Fisheries 2008).

Natural Heritage Rank: S2—Imperiled (NatureServe Explorer 2006).

Habitat Conditions: In Louisiana, Gull-billed Terns nest primarily on barrier beaches, saltmarsh shell berms, and dredged-material islands, and are almost always in close association with Black Skimmers (Portnoy 1977). Dredged-material islands that receive regular seasonal deposits of dredged-material were thought to be increasingly important to nesting Gull-billed Terns and other species (Leberg et al. 1995). Islands in inland lakes and artificial substrates, such as gravel rooftops, are used infrequently. Gull-billed Terns forage over coastal marshes, canals, ponds, and lakes (Lowery 1974, R. D. Purrington, pers. comm.).

Threats: Inundation of estuarine and barrier islands by high or storm tides and loss of nesting habitat as a result of vegetation succession adversely impact nesting success. Human disturbance is believed responsible for the premature desertion of rooftop colonies in 2004 (R. D. Purrington, pers. comm.).

Table A-4. Number of breeding pairs of Gull-billed Terns at colonies along the coast of Louisiana, 1976, 1990–1999 and 2001. Dash (—) indicates data are insufficient to discern site availability, occupancy, or extent of survey coverage for a particular site and year. Topographic quad names follow the Louisiana Natural Heritage Program (LNHP) colony identification numbers. Data from Martin and Lester 1990, Michot et al. 2004, Portnoy 1977, G. D. Lester, pers. comm.

Colony	1976	1990	1991	1992	1993	1994	1995	1996	1997	1998	1999	2001
Iberia Parish												
LNHP 439-Bayou Lucien	—	—	—	—	—	10	100	40	10	50	100	150
Plaquemines Parish												
LNHP 040-Black Bay South	—	0	0	0	0	0	0	0	0	0	0	20
LNHP 082-Grand Gosier I.	—	0	0	0	0	0	0	0	20	0	0	0
LNHP 083-Grand Gosier I.	—	8	0	0	0	0	0	0	0	0	0	0
LNHP 176-Stake Is.	—	0	0	0	0	0	0	100	30	0	0	0
LNHP 361-South Pass	—	—	0	0	0	40	0	0	0	0	0	0
LNHP 393-South Pass	—	—	0	0	0	0	0	3	20	100	100	0
LNHP 469-South Pass	—	—	0	0	0	0	0	0	10	0	0	0
LNHP 524-Taylor Pass	—	—	0	0	0	0	0	0	0	420	0	0
LNHP 545-Taylor Pass	—	—	0	0	0	0	0	0	0	0	20	0
LNHP 546-Taylor Pass	—	—	0	0	0	0	0	0	0	0	20	0
Colony #603037	6	—	—	—	—	—	—	—	—	—	—	—
Terrebonne Parish												
LNHP 055-Cat I. Pass	—	0	0	0	0	0	0	0	10	0	0	0
LNHP 059-Central Isles Dernieres	—	0	0	0	0	0	0	0	60	50	0	0
LNHP 161-Point Au Fer	—	0	0	0	0	0	0	0	60	0	0	0
LNHP 263-Point Au Fer NE	—	150	0	0	0	0	0	0	0	0	0	0
LNHP 440-Jacko Bay	—	—	—	—	—	—	—	—	—	—	—	145
LNHP 555-Oyster Bayou	—	—	0	0	0	0	0	0	20	0	0	0
LNHP 556-Central Isles Dernieres	—	—	0	0	0	0	0	0	6	0	0	0
St. Bernard Parish												
LNHP 181-Three Mile Bay	0	0	0	0	0	0	0	0	2	0	0	0
Colony #590008	20	—	—	—	—	—	—	—	—	—	—	—
St. Mary Parish												
LNHP 266-Point Au Fer NE	—	0	0	0	50	0	0	0	0	0	0	0
LNHP 357-Point Au Fer NE	—	—	0	0	0	100	100	0	0	0	0	0
LNHP 460-Point Au Fer NE	—	—	0	300	200	0	0	0	0	0	0	0
LNHP 461-Point Au Fer NE	—	—	0	0	400	0	0	0	0	0	0	0
LNHP 462-Point Au Fer NE	—	—	0	0	0	140	200	0	0	500	350	125
LNHP 493-Point Au Fer NE	—	—	30	50	0	0	0	0	0	0	0	0
LNHP 494-Point Au Fer NE	—	—	0	0	0	0	0	30	0	0	0	0
Colony #602007	16	—	—	—	—	—	—	—	—	—	—	—
Colony #602008	112	—	—	—	—	—	—	—	—	—	—	—
Vermilion Parish												
LNHP 060-Fearman Lake	—	3	0	0	0	0	0	0	0	0	0	0
Totals	154	161	30	350	650	290	400	173	248	1120	590	440

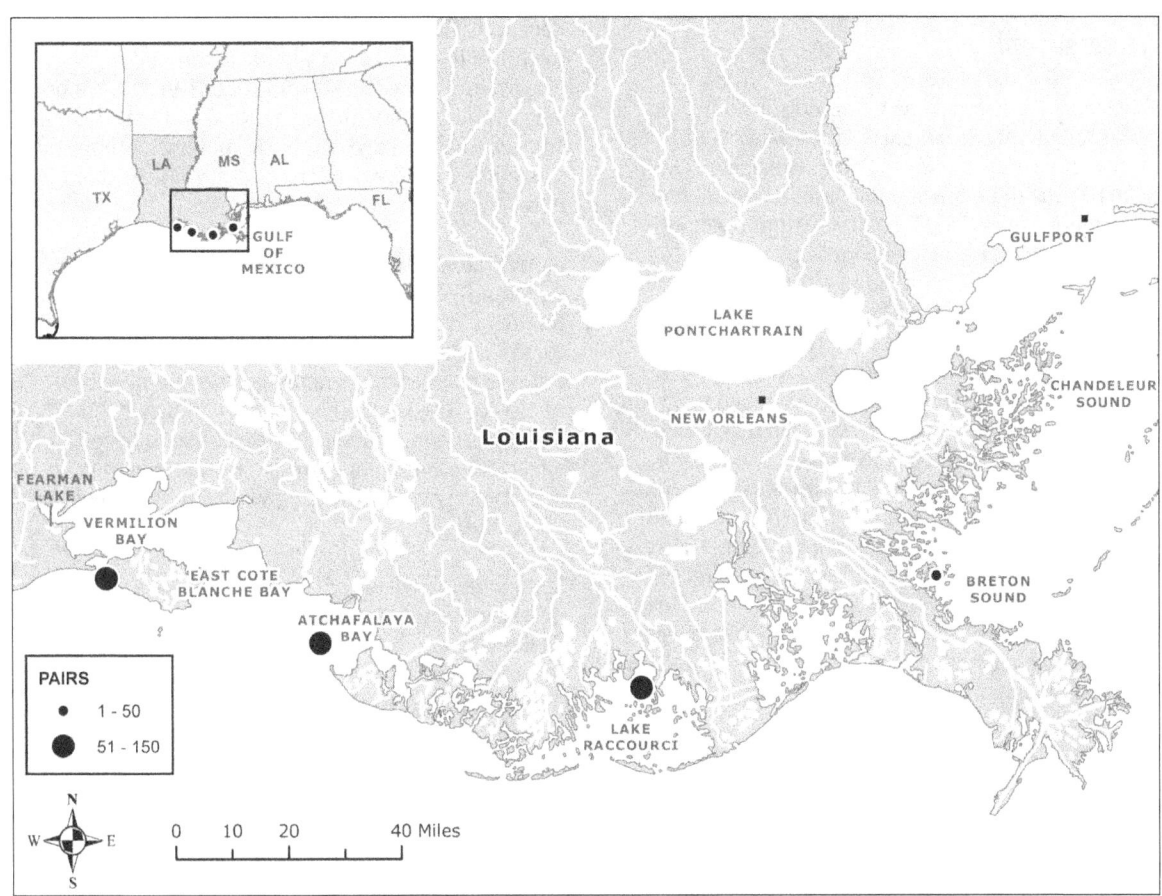

Figure A-4. Locations and sizes of Gull-billed Tern colonies in Louisiana, 2001.

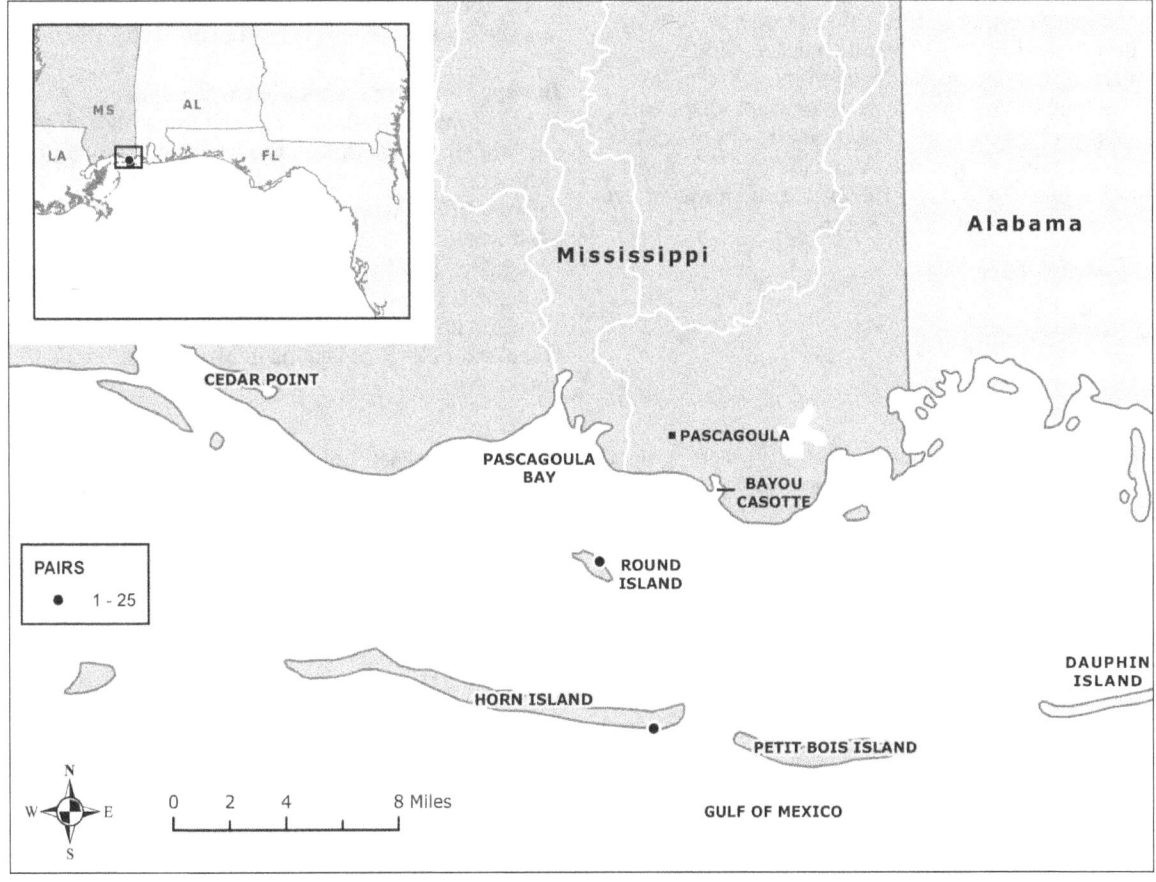

Figure A-5. Locations and sizes of Gull-billed Tern colonies in Mississippi, 2003.

Mississippi

Summary: Mississippi has a limited shoreline and holds only a few dozen pairs of breeding Gull-billed Terns. Turcotte and Watts (1999) considered Gull-billed Terns to be uncommon summer residents breeding on islands off the Mississippi coast. Burleigh (1945) reported them as present and nesting on Petit Bois Island in 1913. The first state specimens of this species from Horn Island were not secured until 1941 (Gandy and Turcotte 1970). On the Mississippi mainland, breeding was first suspected in June 1955, but not confirmed until May 1960 at Bayou Casotte in Jackson County. Since this record, Gull-billed Terns have nested on various dredged-material islands in the Mississippi Sound and Pascagoula River channel (Turcotte and Watts 1999). There is one inland record of a single bird feeding over flooded fields in Lowndes County in July (Turcotte and Watts 1999). The most important recently occupied colony sites are on three barrier or dredged-material islands, East Horn, Round, and Sand islands, in marshes along large river channels (Fig. A-5).

Population Trends: Gull-billed Terns were not historically abundant in Mississippi. Up to three pairs were believed to be nesting in 1960. In 1962, 11 pairs were nesting near Pascagoula, while an undetermined number of pairs were also present on Grand Island in the Mississippi Sound (Gandy and Turcotte 1970). Clapp and Buckley's (1984) report of 62 pairs nesting in 1983 conflicts with reports by Turcotte and Watts (1999) and Jackson (1983) of "as many as 31 nests on dredged-material" in the Pascagoula River for that year; perhaps Clapp and Buckley (1984) confused the total number of adults with the number of nests. A maximum of 150 pairs bred at one site in 2004 (Tables 2, A-5); however, two to five pairs per site is more typical.

Research/Monitoring: No research studies specific to Gull-billed Terns have been conducted in Mississippi. Since 1994, Gull-billed Terns have been surveyed annually during general waterbird colony surveys. Efforts are currently underway to produce a Breeding Bird Atlas for the state (M. A. Goodman, pers. comm.).

Conservation/Management Activities: East Horn and Sand islands fall under the jurisdiction of the National Park Service, while the Round Island colony occurs on state-owned lands which provide relative protection from private development. Access to Sand Island is restricted during the nesting season, reducing disturbance to breeding birds. No other conservation or management activities specific to nesting waterbirds occur at these sites.

State Status: Species of Greatest Conservation Need (Mississippi Department of Wildlife, Fisheries and Parks 2005).

Natural Heritage Rank: S2—Imperiled (NatureServe Explorer 2006).

Habitat Conditions: In Mississippi, Gull-billed Terns nest on dredged-material islands in marshes of large river channels and on barrier islands. Nesting substrates include beach dunes and bare dredged-material. Gull-billed Terns often nests with other terns and Black Skimmers. In Mississippi, Gull-billed Terns feed over open areas such as airports, marshes, and beaches (Turcotte and Watts 1999).

Threats: Unknown. Vegetation succession on dredged-material islands may limit nesting habitat availability. Conflicts with the timing of deposition of new dredged-material may interfere with colony establishment or adversely affect established colonies, as was documented for Least, Royal (*Thalasseus maximus*) and Sandwich (*T. sandvicensis*) terns and potentially Gull-billed Terns on an unnamed dredged-material island near Horn and Petit Bois islands in Mississippi Sound (Jackson 1983).

Table A-5. Number of Gull-billed Tern breeding pairs at colonies in Jackson County, Mississippi, 1988–2004 (M. P. Stevens, pers. comm.). Dash (—) indicates data are insufficient to discern site availability, occupancy, or extent of survey coverage for a particular site and year.

Colony	1988	1989	1990	1991	1992	1993	1994	1995	1996	1997	1998	1999	2000	2001	2002	2003	2004
East Horn I.	—	—	—	—	—	—	0	—	0	0	0	0	0	0	0	1	0
Round I.	—	—	—	—	—	—	—	0	—	0	0	—	0	0	0	1	0
Sand I.	—	—	—	—	—	—	0	—	2	1	0	—	0	—	5	0	150
Totals	—	—	—	—	—	—	0	0	0	1	0	0	0	0	5	2	150

New Jersey and New York

Summary: Small, but increasing numbers of Gull-billed Terns occupy estuarine islands, dunes, and shell bars on the New Jersey coast. The species is considered an uncommon summer resident in New Jersey (Sibley 1993); the highest count in recent years was 92 pairs among five colonies in 2001 (Table A-6). Nesting occurs from Ocean County south to Cape May County, generally on or near the Forsythe NWR (Fig. A-6). The small and fairly recently established colonies on southwestern Long Island, New York, represent the northernmost breeding sites of *G. n. aranea*. Bull (1964) considered Gull-billed Terns to be rare and irregular fall visitors on the southern coast of Long Island. Two pairs of Gull-billed Terns first colonized New York at Black Banks Island near Jones Beach State Park in Nassau County in 1975 (Buckley et al. 1975). Currently, a few pairs now breed on islands off southwestern Long Island (Fig. A-7; Table A-7).

Population Trends: A pair of Gull-billed Terns apparently colonized southern New Jersey (at Stone Harbor) by 1926 (Sibley 1993). In 1977, 18 to 19 pairs nested in the state (Erwin 1979). Over the last few decades, the species seems to have experienced a moderate increase in the number of breeding pairs in New Jersey as 92 pairs bred in 2001 (Fig. A-6; Tables 2, A-6). Gull-billed Terns colonized New York in 1975 and remained at very low numbers through the 1990s. A maximum of 11 pairs bred at three sites in New York in 2003 (Fig. A-7; Tables 2, A-7).

Research/Monitoring: No research studies specific to Gull-billed Terns have been conducted in either state. Aerial censuses of breeding larids are conducted via helicopter on an irregular basis in New Jersey. Since the late 1970s, coastal censuses from Point Pleasant south to Cape May, which included counts of Gull-billed Terns, have been conducted in 1977, 1978, 1979, 1983, 1985, 1989, and 1995 and were extended north to Sea Bright in 2001 and 2004 (C. D. Jenkins, pers. comm.). The Long Island Colonial Waterbird Monitoring Project conducts annual censuses of terns in the Long Island/New York City region of New York (M. R. Wasilco, pers. comm.). During these surveys all breeding species are tallied, nest contents recorded, and nest locations mapped on aerial photos or maps of each site, and information on site characteristics, ownership, disturbance factors, predation levels, and management needs are recorded (M. R. Wasilco, pers. comm.)

Table A-6. Number of breeding pairs of Gull-billed Terns at colonies in New Jersey, 1977, 1985, 1995, and 2001 (Erwin and Korschgen 1979, R. Andrews and C. D. Jenkins, pers. comm.).

Colony	1977	1985	1995	2001
Ocean Co.				
Chadwick Marsh	5	0	0	0
Atlantic Co.				
Elder Island-Brigantine Channel	8	1	2	0
Main Marsh Thorofare	0	15	4	0
Oceanville 61470	0	0	0	40
Oceanville 62481	0	0	0	13
Oceanville 65520	0	0	0	10
Oceanville 66530	0	0	0	2
Oyster Thorofare	5	0	0	0
Simpkins Thorofare	0	1	12	27
Cape May Co.				
Jarvis Sound-Wildwood Crest	1	0	0	0
Totals	19	17	18	92

Conservation/Management Activities: No active conservation or management measures are currently conducted. Of the 12 colony sites in New Jersey where Gull-billed Terns are known to have nested, nearly 70% occur within federal or state wildlife management areas and are relatively safe from development. All Gull-billed Tern nesting sites in New York occur on public lands under local jurisdictions with no specific conservation or management actions directed toward their populations.

State Status: No status in New Jersey or New York.

Natural Heritage Rank: S1 – Critically imperiled in both states (NatureServe Explorer 2006).

Habitat Conditions: In both states, Gull-billed Terns nest primarily on estuarine islands composed of marsh wrack, and occasionally on sand dunes and shell bars. In New York, Gull-billed Terns also nest on sand and shell substrates on barrier islands and on dredged-material islands.

Threats: Sea level rise and potential inundation of low-lying colony sites, increases in gull populations, and human disturbance on beaches may limit reproductive success in New Jersey. In New York, reduced suitability of nesting sites due to beach development, increased levels of human disturbance, and increases in gull breeding populations (Buckley and Buckley 1984) appear to be the main threats to Gull-billed Terns.

Table A-7. Number of breeding pairs of Gull-billed Terns at colonies in New York, 1975, 1984–1999, and 2001–2003. Dash (—) indicates data are insufficient to discern site availability, occupancy, or extent of survey coverage for a particular site and year. Data from Buckley et al. 1975, Sommers et al. 1994, 2001, M. R. Wasilco, pers. comm.

Colony	1975	1984	1985	1986	1987	1988	1989	1990	1991	1992	1993	1994	1995	1996	1997	1998	1999	2001	2002	2003
Long Island, Suffolk Co																				
Cedar Beach	—	1	0	0	0	0	0	0	0	0	0	0	0	0	0	0	0	0	0	0
Long Island, Nassau Co																				
Cinder Island Group	—	—	—	1	0	1	1	0	0	2	1	1	0	2	4	4	5	4	1	1
Cuba Island Group	—	—	1	1	0	1	1	1	1	1	0	0	0	0	0	1	0	0	1	0
Deep Creek Meadow	—	—	—	—	—	1	0	0	0	0	0	0	0	0	0	0	0	0	0	0
East Channel Island/Garrett Marsh	—	1	0	0	0	0	0	0	0	0	0	0	0	0	0	0	0	1	1	8
Gull Island/Parsonage Isl. Group	—	—	—	—	—	—	—	—	—	—	1	0	0	0	0	0	0	1	0	0
Jones Beach	2	0	0	0	0	0	0	0	0	0	0	0	0	0	0	0	0	0	0	0
Lawrence Marsh	—	—	—	—	1	0	0	0	0	0	0	0	2	0	0	0	0	0	0	0
Long Meadow Island	—	—	—	—	—	—	—	—	1	0	1	0	0	1	1	0	1	1	0	2
Middle Line Island	—	—	—	—	1	0	0	0	0	0	0	0	0	0	0	0	0	0	0	0
Neds Island	—	1	1	0	0	0	0	0	0	0	0	0	0	0	0	0	0	0	0	0
Totals	2	3	2	2	2	3	2	1	2	3	3	1	2	3	4	5	6	6	3	11

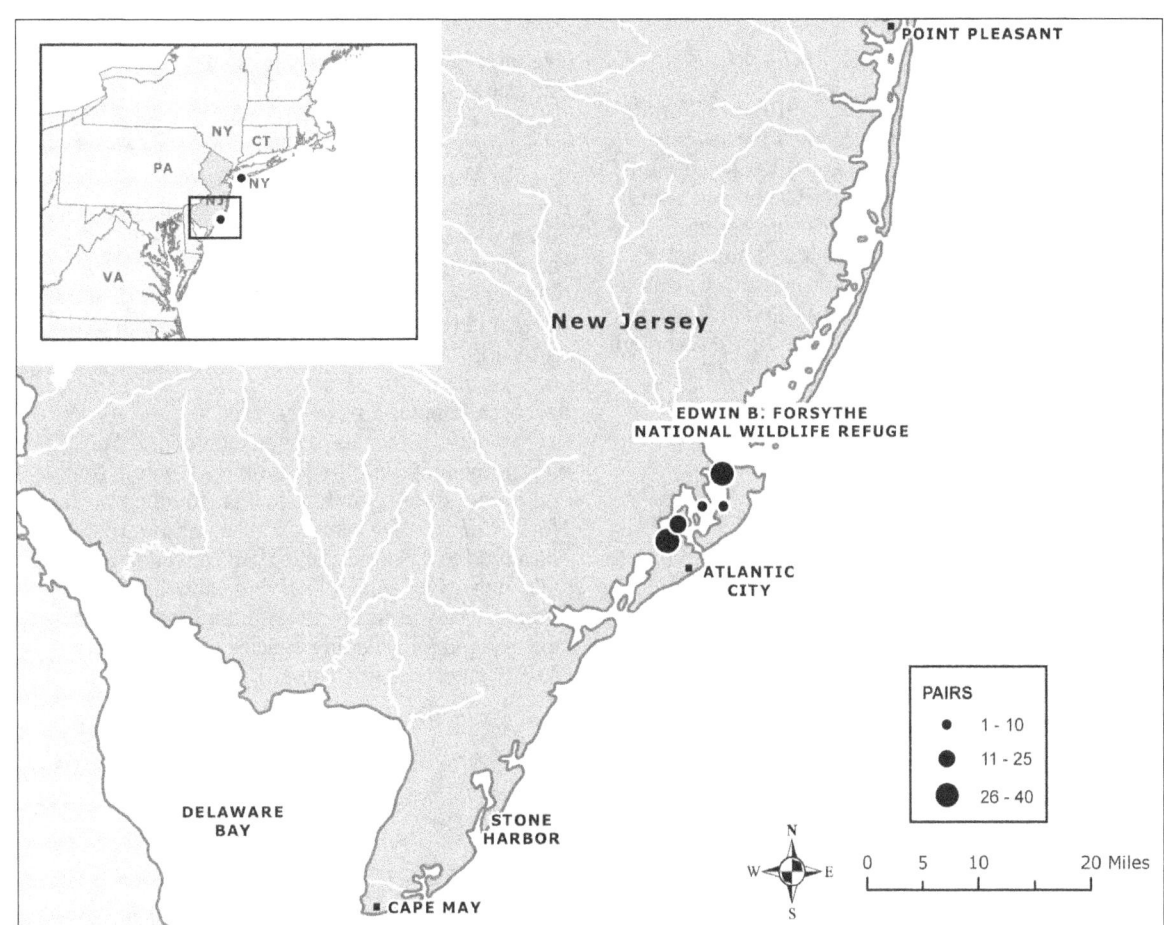

Figure A-6. Locations and sizes of Gull-billed Tern colonies in New Jersey, 2001.

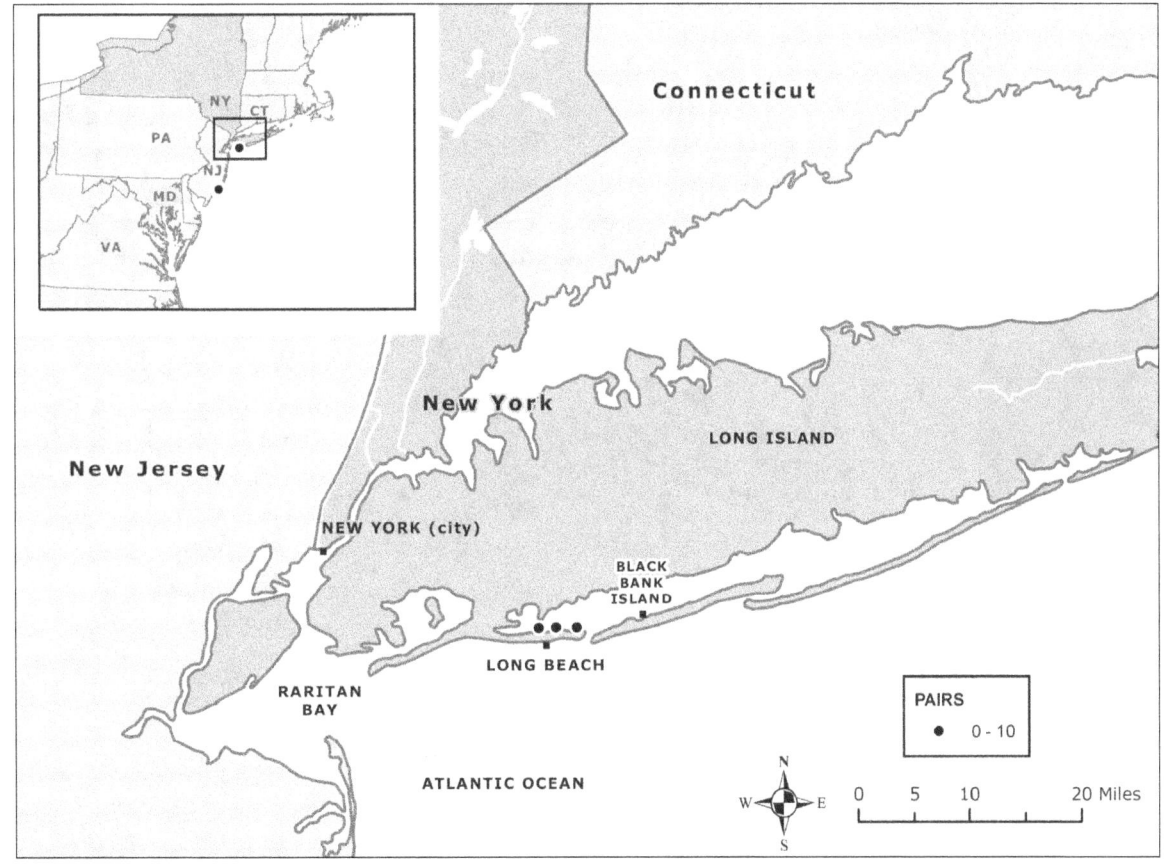

Figure A-7. Locations and sizes of Gull-billed Tern colonies in New York, 2003.

North Carolina

Summary: In 1909, Pearson et al. (1919) considered Gull-billed Terns to be rare breeders in the state. The species has become more abundant since then and nesting is more widespread (Parnell and Soots 1979). Gull-billed Terns are primarily summer residents and are reported to nest at a number of locations along the Atlantic coast of North Carolina from Roanoke Sound south to the Cape Fear River (Clapp et al. 1983, Parnell and Soots 1979). Although the number of breeding pairs has declined from 1977 levels, it has remained stable, at around 200 to 250 pairs, over the last decade (Table A-8).

Population Trends: Long-term trends are difficult to discern as comprehensive state-wide censuses did not begin until the late 1970s. Parnell and Soots (1979) reported 621 Gull-billed Tern nests among 21 colony sites in 1977. Parnell and McCrimmon (1984) later reported that the peak number of nests (presumed to equal the peak number of pairs) at nine colony sites was 268 in 1977 and 223 in 1983. The peak number of nests reported by Parnell et al.

(1995) for 1993 was 155 at 10 colony sites. During this later census, the vast majority of nests were on Pamlico Sound in Dare, Hyde, and Carteret counties (Parnell et al. 1995). In 2001, 258 pairs were found breeding among seven colony sites (Fig. A-8; Tables 2, A-8). Although the state population size is small, it appears to have been relatively stable over the last two decades. Recent census results indicate a reduction in the number of colony sites, with a shift in the center of abundance away from the Cape Fear River and toward the northeastern portion of the state (Fig. A-8).

Research/Monitoring: No research studies specific to Gull-billed Terns have been conducted. The North Carolina Wildlife Resources Commission and cooperators (North Carolina Audubon Society, North Carolina Division of Parks and Recreation, National Park Service, and USFWS) conduct coast-wide surveys of colonial nesting waterbirds every two to three years. These are mainly ground-based surveys and all breeding species are counted (S. E. Cameron, pers. comm.).

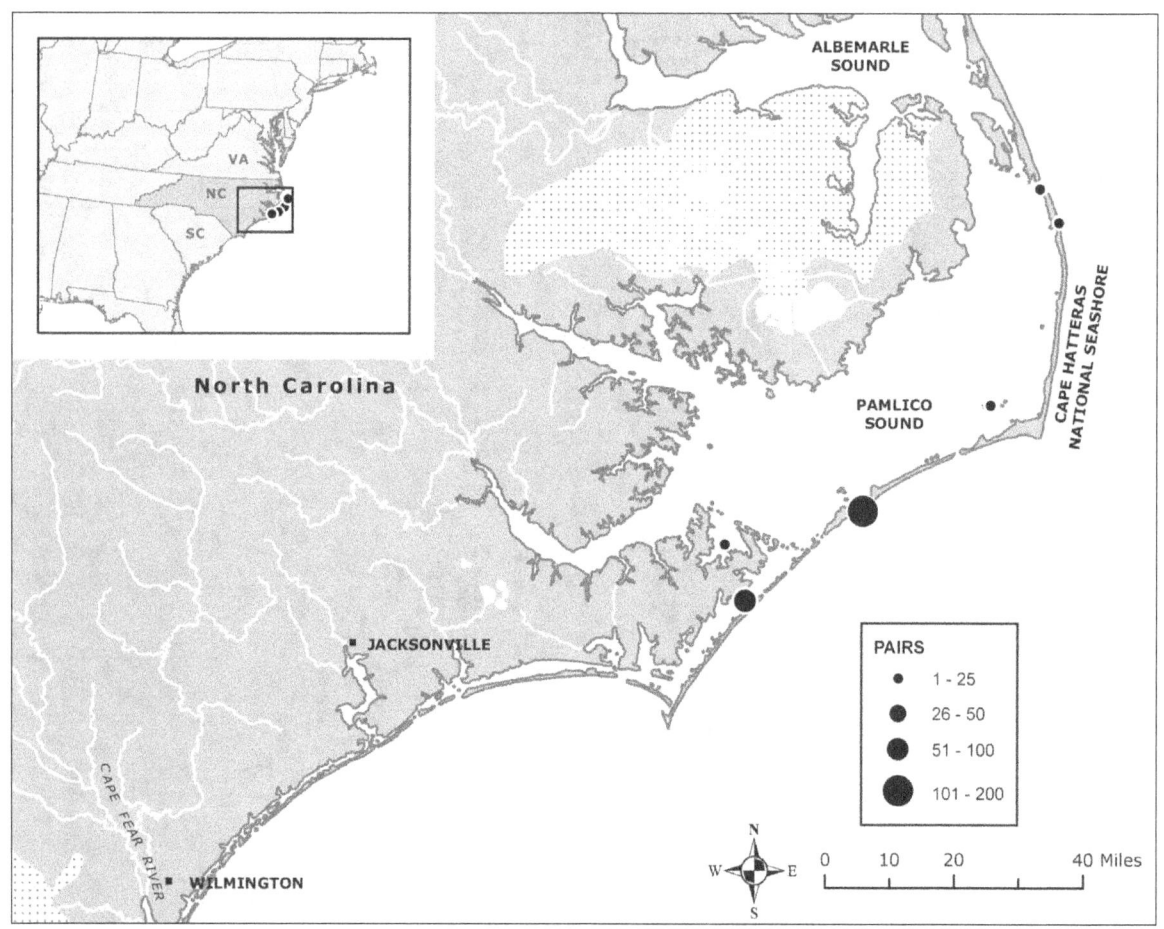

Figure A-8. Locations and sizes of Gull-billed Tern colonies in North Carolina, 2001.

Table A-8. Number of breeding pairs of Gull-billed Terns at colonies in North Carolina, 1976–1977, 1983–1993, 1995, 1997, 1999, and 2001. Surveys conducted statewide in 1976, 1977, 1985, and 1993 through 2001 were comprehensive. Dash (—) indicates data are insufficient to discern site availability, occupancy, or extent of survey coverage for a particular site and year. Data from Parnell and Soots 1979, Parnell et al. 1995, Portnoy et al. 1981, D. H. Allen, pers. comm.

Colony	1976	1977	1983	1984	1985	1986	1987	1988	1989	1990	1991	1992	1993	1995	1997	1999	2001
Currituck Co																	
Brant Island	29	100	64	0	0	0	0	2	0	0	0	0	0	0	0	0	0
Dare Co																	
Clam Shoal	—	—	—	—	—	—	—	—	—	—	—	—	—	—	—	—	24
Dot Island	0	36	7	0	6	0	0	—	—	—	—	—	—	—	—	—	—
Hatteras Beach Site 2	0	0	4	0	0	0	0	1	—	—	—	—	—	—	—	—	—
Hatteras Inlet (06-11)	10	—	—	—	—	—	—	—	—	—	—	—	—	—	—	—	—
Hatteras Inlet (09-03)	60	—	—	—	—	—	—	—	—	—	—	—	—	—	—	—	—
Hatteras Inlet (09-04)	1	—	—	—	—	—	—	—	—	—	—	—	—	—	—	—	—
Hatteras Inlet, Northside Beach	0	0	3	16	7	0	0	0	0	0	4	0	0	7	79	0	0
Old Dot Island	—	8	—	—	—	—	—	—	—	—	—	—	—	—	—	—	—
Old House Channel, Island L	—	4	0	0	15	0	0	0	0	0	0	0	0	0	6	0	0
Old House Channel, Island MN (06-08)	10	21	0	0	0	0	0	0	0	0	0	0	0	102	0	0	0
Oregon Inlet Beach, South	—	—	—	—	—	—	—	—	—	—	—	—	—	—	27	6	22
Oregon Inlet Shoal	—	—	—	—	—	—	—	—	—	—	—	—	—	—	—	—	1
Oregon Inlet, Island B	—	22	4	—	—	—	—	—	—	—	—	—	—	—	—	—	—
Pea Island Beach, Cedar Hammock	—	—	—	—	—	—	—	—	—	—	—	—	—	—	—	—	—
Pea Island Beach, Pole Shed	—	—	—	—	—	—	—	—	—	—	—	—	—	—	—	—	5
Pea Island, South Pond	—	—	—	—	—	—	—	—	—	—	—	—	1	—	—	—	—
Roanoke Sound, Island G	8	—	—	—	—	—	—	—	—	—	—	—	—	—	—	—	—
Roanoke Sound, Island H	—	—	29	—	—	—	—	—	—	—	—	—	—	—	—	—	—
Sand Shoal Island	—	—	—	—	—	—	—	47	11	49	100	50	26	—	—	—	—
UNI, Old House Channel	—	4	—	—	—	—	—	—	—	—	—	—	—	—	—	—	—
UNI, Pea Island, North Pond 1	—	—	—	13	—	—	—	—	—	—	—	—	—	—	—	—	—
UNI, Stumpy Point Bay	32	4	15	—	—	—	—	—	—	—	—	—	—	—	—	—	—
Unnamed (03-12)	13	—	—	—	—	—	—	—	—	—	—	—	—	—	—	—	—
Unnamed (06-07)	5	—	—	—	—	—	—	—	—	—	—	—	—	—	—	—	—
Wells Island	—	—	—	—	—	—	—	—	—	—	—	10	41	0	0	0	0

Colony	1976	1977	1983	1984	1985	1986	1987	1988	1989	1990	1991	1992	1993	1995	1997	1999	2001
Hyde Co																	
Big Foot Island	—	—	—	—	—	—	—	—	—	—	—	—	—	25	4	—	—
Hog Island Reef	5	—	—	—	—	—	—	—	—	—	—	—	—	—	—	—	—
North Rock Island	16	—	—	—	—	—	—	4	—	—	—	—	—	—	—	—	—
Ocracoke Flats	—	—	—	—	—	—	—	—	—	—	—	—	—	—	—	—	—
Ocracoke Inlet Beach, North	0	27	—	48	146	4	27	0	0	9	0	0	0	15	5	103	108
Ocracoke Inlet, Natural Shoal	—	—	—	—	—	—	—	—	8	—	—	—	—	—	—	—	—
Shell Castle Island, West	—	—	—	—	—	—	—	—	—	—	—	—	—	—	3	—	—
UNI, Hatteras Ferry Channel 1	—	—	—	—	—	—	—	—	—	—	2	—	—	—	—	—	—
UNI, Hatteras Ferry Channel 2	—	13	—	—	—	—	—	—	—	—	—	—	—	—	—	—	—
Carteret Co.																	
Beaufort Causeway	—	—	—	—	—	—	—	—	—	—	23	—	—	—	—	—	—
Bogue Sound (22-08)	5	—	—	—	—	—	—	—	—	—	—	—	—	—	—	—	—
Bogue Sound (22-40)	2	—	—	—	—	—	—	—	—	—	—	—	—	—	—	—	—
Bottle Run Point	12	0	0	0	0	0	0	3	0	0	0	0	19	29	0	0	0
Cape Point	0	0	0	32	0	33	11	0	16	23	0	0	11	36	0	0	0
Cape Point, South Beach	—	—	—	—	—	—	—	25	—	—	—	—	—	—	—	—	—
Core Banks Beach, North, Drum Inlet	0	2	—	—	—	—	—	—	—	—	—	—	—	—	—	—	—
Core Banks Beach, South, Drum Inlet	0	0	3	0	—	0	0	21	0	0	0	0	—	0	1	0	0
Core Banks, Power Squadron Spit	—	—	—	—	—	—	—	4	0	0	0	16	—	—	—	—	—
Drum Inlet, North	0	52	—	—	—	—	—	2	—	—	—	—	—	—	—	—	—
Harbor Island	—	—	—	—	—	—	—	—	25	0	0	0	1	0	0	0	0
Morgan Island	—	—	6	—	—	—	—	10	—	—	—	—	—	—	—	—	—
New Drum Inlet, Shoal	—	—	—	—	—	—	—	—	—	—	—	—	1	28	—	—	—
New Dump Island	39	85	0	0	0	0	0	0	0	0	0	0	0	0	0	20	87
Newport River, Annex	1	—	—	—	—	—	—	—	—	—	—	—	—	—	—	—	—
Newstump Point	—	—	—	—	—	—	—	—	—	—	—	—	10	—	—	—	—
Old Dump Island	—	—	5	—	—	—	—	5	1	—	—	—	—	—	—	—	—
Portsmouth Island	41	—	—	—	—	—	—	3	—	—	—	—	—	—	—	—	—
Sand Bag Island	—	—	—	—	—	—	—	—	—	—	—	—	—	—	—	—	—
Shackleford Point	—	—	—	—	—	—	—	16	—	—	—	—	37	—	—	—	—
Shell Island	0	1	0	0	0	0	0	0	0	0	0	0	2	0	0	0	0
Swash Inlet, Beach	—	15	0	0	0	0	0	0	0	0	0	0	0	0	1	0	0

Table A-8. (cont'd)

Colony	1976	1977	1983	1984	1985	1986	1987	1988	1989	1990	1991	1992	1993	1995	1997	1999	2001
Tump Island	—	—	—	—	—	—	—	—	—	2	0	0	0	0	0	0	11
UNI, Adjacent Lighthouse Bay (17-03)	9	2	—	—	—	—	—	—	—	—	—	—	—	—	—	—	—
UNI, Back Sound 4	—	—	—	—	—	—	—	—	—	—	—	—	—	4	—	—	—
UNI, Core Sound 3	—	2	—	—	—	—	—	—	—	—	—	—	—	—	—	—	—
UNI, Swansboro 6 (23-10)	2	0	0	0	0	0	0	2	—	—	—	—	—	—	—	—	—
Unnamed (15-09)	13	—	—	—	—	—	—	—	—	—	—	—	—	—	—	—	—
Unnamed (22-02)	19	—	—	—	—	—	—	—	—	—	—	—	—	—	—	—	—
Unnamed (22-04)	1	—	—	—	—	—	—	—	—	—	—	—	—	—	—	—	—
Westend-Bird Shoal (20-03)	21	6	0	0	0	0	0	2	—	—	—	—	—	—	—	—	—
Onslow Co.																	
UNI, New River Channel 3	—	—	—	—	—	—	—	4	—	—	—	—	—	—	—	—	—
Pender Co																	
Old Topsail Inlet, North	4	0	0	0	0	0	0	0	0	0	0	0	0	0	0	1	0
Rich Inlet, Northside	—	—	—	—	—	—	—	—	1	—	—	—	—	—	—	—	—
Unnamed (29-36)	17	—	—	—	—	—	—	—	—	—	—	—	—	—	—	—	—
New Hanover Co.																	
Ferry Slip Island	—	—	—	—	—	—	—	—	—	—	—	5	0	1	0	0	0
Fort Fisher Beach	—	—	—	—	—	—	—	10	6	6	0	0	0	0	0	0	0
Mason Inlet, Northside	—	—	—	—	—	—	—	—	—	9	—	—	—	—	—	—	—
Masonboro Island	7	—	—	—	—	—	—	—	—	—	—	—	—	—	—	—	—
UNI, Cape Fear River (39-33)	32	0	52	—	—	—	—	—	—	—	—	—	—	—	—	—	—
Bird I.	27	—	—	—	—	—	—	—	—	—	—	—	—	—	—	—	—
South Pelican Island	0	34	0	0	0	0	0	0	0	0	0	0	7	0	11	24	0
UNI, Anderson Landing	—	—	41	—	—	—	—	—	—	—	—	—	—	—	—	—	—
UNI, Monks Island, Bowen-Point	—	19	0	—	—	—	—	—	—	—	—	—	—	—	—	—	—
UNI, Old Brunswick (39-26)	87	164	—	—	—	—	—	—	—	3	—	—	—	—	—	—	—
Unnamed (39-29)	40	—	—	—	—	—	—	—	—	—	—	—	—	—	—	—	—
Assignation unknown	27	—	—	—	—	—	—	—	—	—	—	—	—	—	—	—	—
Totals	595	621	233	109	174	37	38	161	68	101	129	81	155	249	137	154	258

Conservation/Management Activities: At least 19 (23%) of the 82 locations where Gull-billed Terns are known to have bred occur within national parks or NWRs and are protected. Protective signage restricting public access occurs at Oregon Inlet Shoal, administered by the USFWS, and Dot Island (S. E. Cameron, pers. comm.). No other management activities specifically directed at nesting Gull-billed Terns are presently conducted at these sites (S. E. Cameron, pers. comm.).

State Status: Threatened (North Carolina Wildlife Resources Commission 2005).

Natural Heritage Rank: S3—Vulnerable (NatureServe Explorer 2006).

Habitat Conditions: In North Carolina, Gull-billed Terns nest primarily on open and bare areas of undiked dredged-material and natural estuarine islands and on coastal beaches. Nesting substrates are most often of mixed sand and shell (Parnell et al. 1995).

Threats: Flooding of low elevation sites is prevalent and occurs at Big Foot Island, Core Banks Beach, Ft. Fisher Beach, Harbor Island, Mason Inlet, Ocracoke Inlet Beach and Shoal, New Drum Inlet, Oregon Inlet Beach and Shoal, and Shell, South Pelican, Tump, and Wells islands. Vegetation succession on dredged-material islands limit nesting habitat. Human disturbances on the outer beaches can severely disrupt nesting colonies (North Carolina Wildlife Resources Commission 2005).

South Carolina

Summary: Sprunt and Chamberlain (1949) considered Gull-billed Terns to be sparse and irregular breeders in South Carolina. The first nests of this species were discovered on Cape Island (at Cape Romain) in 1929 (Sprunt and Chamberlain 1949). Gull-billed Terns nest locally along the central coast from Cape Romain and Bull's Bay south to the Savannah River with most nesting occurring presently in the Cape Romain area.

Population Trends: Although figures in published reports sometimes conflict, state numbers appear to be relatively stable over the last 30 years (Tables 2, A-9). Blus and Stafford (1980) reported an annual maximum of 340 nests from up to 10 colony sites during their 1969–1975 study. Clapp et al's (1983) map depiction of 12 breeding birds in 1976 near the Savannah River conflicts with Clapp and Buckley's (1984) estimate of 231 pairs in 1976. Gull-billed Terns in South Carolina exhibit considerable inter-annual variation; from 1990–2003 the number of pairs ranged from 109 to 414 at four to 10 colony sites (Fig. A-9; Tables 2, A-9; J. S. Calver, pers. comm.)

Research/Monitoring: No research studies specific to Gull-billed Terns have been conducted. Field work for a breeding bird atlas was conducted between 1988 and 1995 but survey coverage for colonial breeding waterbirds was inadequate to assess state numbers (South Carolina Department of Natural Resources 2005). Censuses of all colonial breeding waterbirds were conducted annually from about 1987–2004.

Conservation/Management Activities: Of the 27 sites where Gull-billed Terns are known to have nested in South Carolina, 12 (54%) occurred on NWRs and two (7%) on State Heritage Sites. In 2004, only nine nesting islands were active, all of which were located in Charleston County on lands administered by the NWR system or the state's Heritage Preserve Program. Management activities include the posting of protective signage and barriers at 18 sites and vegetation removal at three dredged-material sites (J. S. Calver, pers. comm.). The Gull-billed Tern is a South Carolina Priority Species with the highest priority ranking (South Carolina Department of Natural Resources 2005).

State Status: Species of Concern (South Carolina Department of Natural Resources 2005).

Table A-9. Number of breeding pairs of Gull-billed Terns at colonies in South Carolina, 1975–1976, 1979, 1986–1990, and 1992–2003 (Portnoy et al. 1981, T. M. Murphy, pers. comm.). Statewide census effort begins about 1987; earliest censuses may not have been comprehensive. Dash (—) indicates data are insufficient to discern site availability, occupancy, or extent of survey coverage for a particular site and year.

Colony	1975	1976	1979	1986	1987	1988	1989	1990	1992	1993	1994	1995	1996	1997	1998	1999	2000	2001	2002	2003
Georgetown Co.																				
Magnolia Beach	—	1	—	—	—	—	—	—	—	—	—	—	—	—	—	—	—	—	—	—
North Is., n. end	—	—	—	—	6	4	—	—	—	—	—	—	—	—	—	—	—	—	—	—
Charleston Co.																				
Bird Key, Bull Bay	7	133	0	0	0	28	35	0	0	0	0	0	0	0	0	0	0	0	0	0
Bird Key, Stono River	—	—	56	30	65	7	0	113	0	0	29	0	0	0	7	0	0	0	0	0
Cape Is., n. end of n. end	—	—	—	—	—	—	—	—	—	—	9	0	0	0	0	0	0	4	0	1
Cape Is., n. end of s. end	—	—	—	—	—	—	—	—	—	—	2	0	0	0	0	0	0	0	2	0
Cape Is., s. end of s. end	—	—	5	8	6	3	5	45	0	0	0	1	0	0	0	0	0	0	0	0
Cape Island	—	—	—	—	—	—	—	—	—	—	—	0	0	6	0	0	0	10	32	0
Castle Pickney	—	—	—	—	—	29	79	63	0	16	0	6	76	68	88	26	0	28	0	47
Crab Bank	—	—	—	—	—	0	0	0	0	0	0	7	5	11	15	20	64	27	0	48
Deveaux Bank	—	—	—	—	23	85	193	10	53	129	61	0	0	0	0	0	0	0	0	0
Kiawah Is., n. end	—	—	—	7	—	0	0	1	0	0	0	4	0	0	0	0	0	0	0	0
Lighthouse Isl.	—	—	—	—	17	0	0	0	0	0	0	0	0	0	0	0	0	0	0	0
Lighthouse Isl., s. end	—	—	—	—	—	—	—	—	—	2	4	1	88	37	2	6	1	5	3	16
Marsh Island	—	—	47	0	38	19	0	0	0	0	10	0	9	0	0	0	12	0	0	0
Raccoon Key	—	—	—	—	26	47	15	8	44	0	31	84	0	0	58	0	15	0	8	0
Raccoon Key, Sandy Pt.	—	—	—	—	—	—	—	—	—	87	0	0	0	13	5	0	0	24	0	21
Skimmer Flats	—	—	—	—	26	30	2	6	0	9	0	3	0	167	36	21	0	0	0	0
White Banks (all isls. combined)	46	12	—	—	—	—	—	—	—	—	—	—	—	—	—	—	—	—	—	—
White Banks, east			0	0	0	0	0	0	0	0	0	0	0	0	1	0	0	0	27	0
White Banks, middle			0	0	0	0	0	0	0	27	40	59	14	25	6	24	0	52	0	0
White Banks, west			0	0	15	0	30	18	0	0	0	0	0	22	0	2	0	21	26	0
Beaufort Co.																				
Egg Bank Isl.	—	—	—	4	0	0	0	14	0	—	0	0	0	0	0	0	0	0	—	—
Joiner Bank	—	—	—	—	—	2	21	136	0	7	—	—	—	—	—	—	—	—	—	—
Jasper Co.																				
Savannah River NWR	—	8	0	0	0	0	0	—	0	—	0	0	0	0	0	0	0	0	0	0
Savannah Spoil, Site 12B	—	—	—	—	—	—	—	—	—	—	—	—	—	—	—	—	—	—	0	28
Savannah Spoil, Site 14B e.	—	—	—	—	—	—	—	—	—	—	—	—	—	—	—	20	164	204	0	78
Savannah Spoil, Site 14B w.	—	—	—	—	—	—	—	—	—	—	—	—	—	—	—	0	0	0	11	0
Totals	53	154	108	49	222	254	380	414	97	277	186	165	192	349	218	119	256	375	109	239

Natural Heritage Rank: SNR—Unranked (NatureServe Explorer 2006).

Habitat Conditions: Gull-billed Terns in South Carolina nest primarily on natural estuarine and barrier islands and on dredged-material islands. Nesting substrates used are primarily sand and shell.

Threats: Presently, breeding Gull-billed Terns in South Carolina may be limited by the availability of suitable nesting locations as the more southerly sites used previously in St. Helena Sound and Port Royal have been lost as a result of erosion (South Carolina Department of Natural Resources 2005). Tidal inundation of the remaining low-lying colony sites, mammalian predation, and human disturbances adversely affect reproductive success in these colonies (J. S. Calver, pers. comm.).

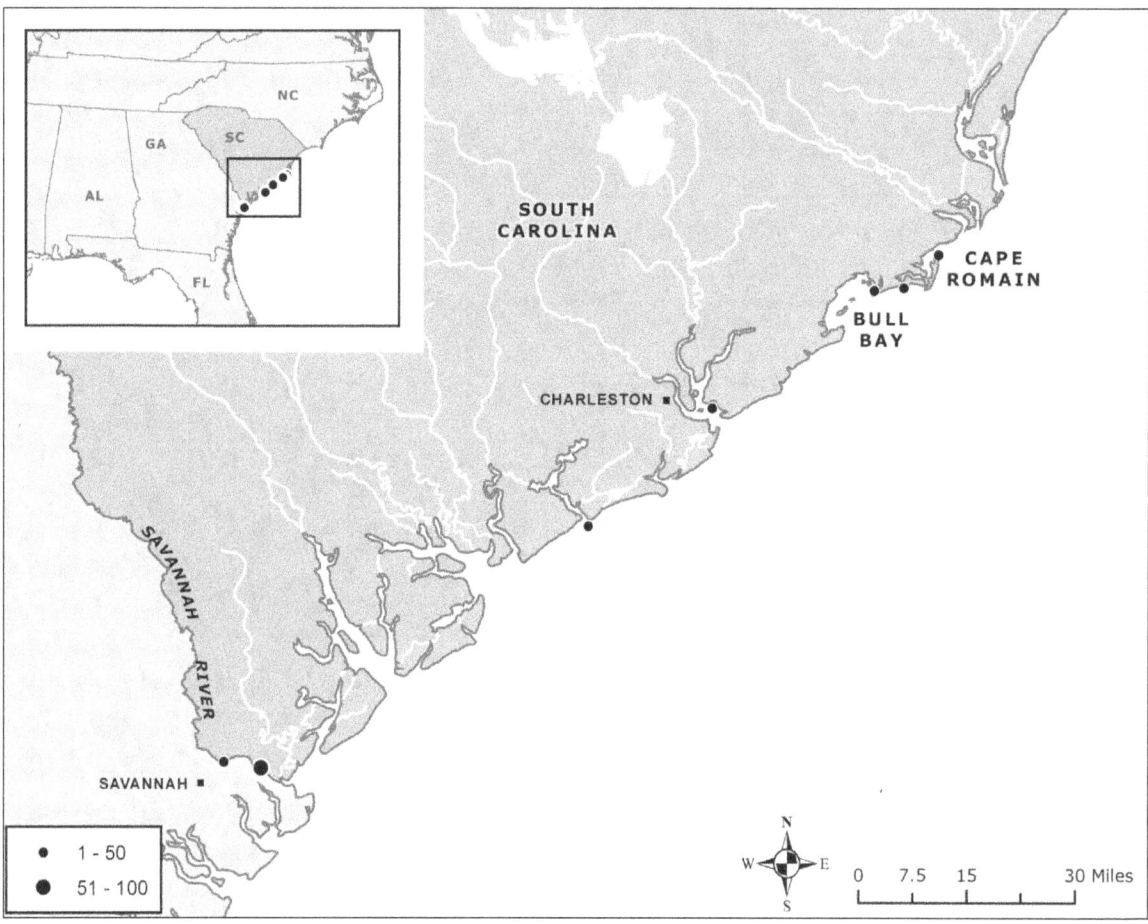

Figure A-9. Locations and sizes of Gull-billed Tern colonies in South Carolina, 2003.

Texas

Summary: The coast of Texas appears to be the core area of abundance for *G. n. aranea*, and the state's breeding population, estimated at over 2000 pairs in recent years, is the highest of any state in the United States or Mexico. Texas colonies have accounted for over 60% of the United States population of *G. n. aranea* during the current decade. Oberholser (1974) considered Gull-billed Terns to be fairly common residents along the Texas coast, nesting locally, but with fewer birds present in winter. Lockwood and Freeman (2004) indicate that this species is common along the coast, though much less numerous in winter. Pemberton (1922) described nesting colonies of Gull-billed Terns near Port Isabel in Cameron County, where he found them to be abundant, possibly ranging into the "many thousands." Since the mid-1990s, colonies containing several hundred nests have formed annually at two inland saline lakes, La Sal Vieja and East Lake, in Willacy County (W. H. Howe and D. Blankinship, pers. comm.). Small resident populations are established farther inland at Falcon Reservoir in Zapata County, and Lake Casa Blanca in Webb County (Lockwood and Freeman 2004).

There are three centers of breeding abundance along the coast (Figs. A-10 through A-12; Tables A-10 through A-12): (1) the upper coast, encompassing Sabine Lake, Galveston Bay, and the Brazoria County Wetlands; (2) the central coast encompassing Lavaca, Matagorda, Aransas, Nueces, San Antonio, and Corpus Christi bays; and (3) the lower coast encompassing the Upper and Lower Laguna Madre. Many of the largest and most consistently occupied colony sites are found in the central and lower coasts (Texas Colonial Waterbird Society 1982) including 12 of the 14 colony sites that contained an annual median of ≥ 51 pairs. The lower, central, and upper coasts contain 38%, 35%, and 27% of all colony sites used in the state, respectively. Consistency of site use was greatest for the lower coast where 38% of 52 sites were used for 15 or more years over the 31 year period. Site use consistency was lower on the central coast (17% of 48 sites), and lowest on the upper coast (3% of 38 sites). From 1990–2003, the three largest coastal colonies occurred most consistently at Mustang Bayou Island in Galveston Bay and Laguna Vista and Green Hill Spoil Island in Lower Laguna Madre. The median numbers of pairs at these sites were 375, 110, and 100 pairs, respectively. In comparison, the median for all 78 sites occupied in any year was 20 pairs. The median colony size rather than the mean is given due to the large annual variation among sites.

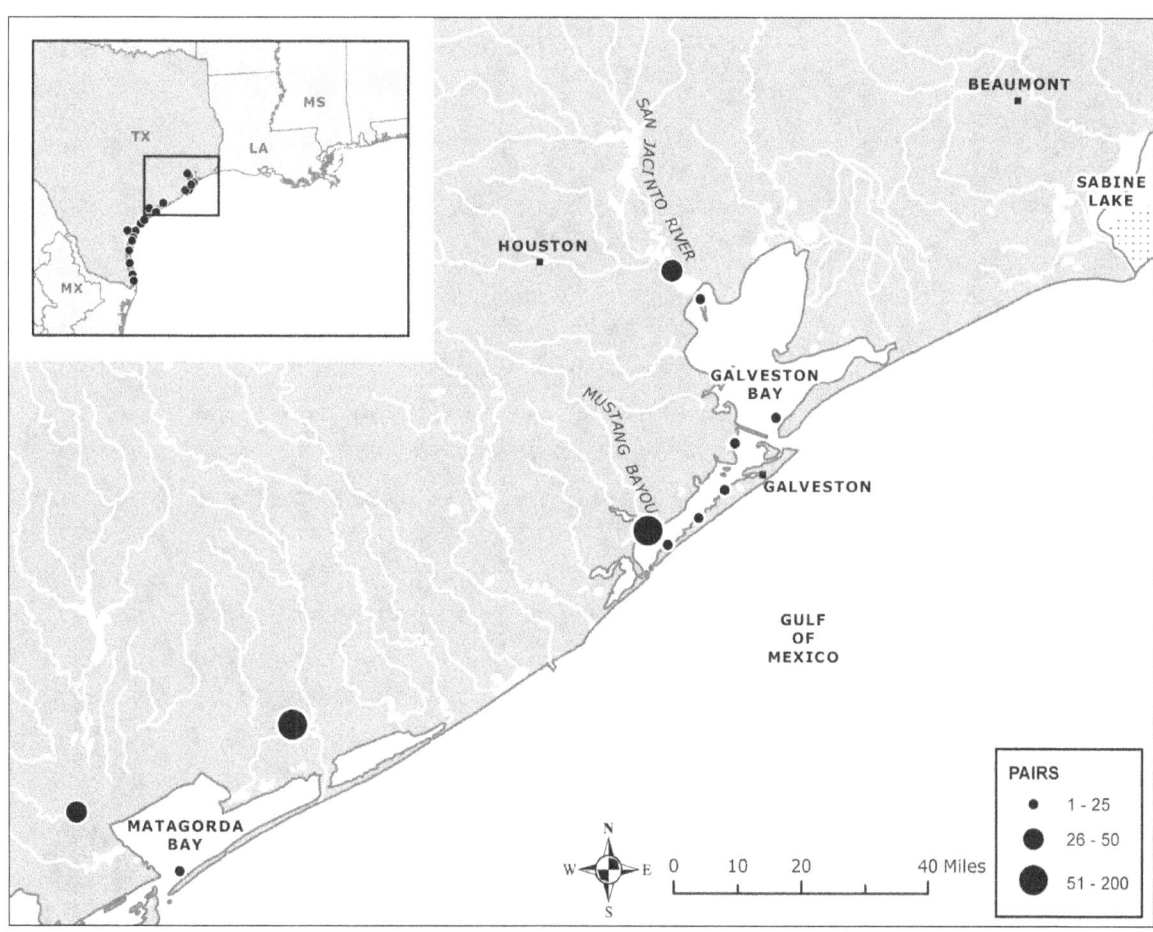

Figure A-10. Locations and sizes of Gull-billed Tern colonies in the upper coast of Texas, 2003.

Colony	1988	1989	1990	1991	1992	1993	1994	1995	1996	1997	1998	1999	2000	2001	2002	2003
Sabine Lake; Jefferson Co.																
Motiva Headquarters	—	—	0	0	0	0	0	0	0	0	0	6	8	0	0	0
Galveston Bay; Chambers Co.																
Atkinson Island	0	0	0	0	0	0	0	0	0	0	0	0	0	0	64	6
Galveston Bay; Harris Co.																
St. Mary's Island	—	—	—	—	—	—	—	—	—	—	—	—	—	—	27	28
Galveston Bay; Galveston Co.																
Bay Harbor Bar	0	0	0	0	0	3	0	0	0	0	1	0	0	0	0	4
Carancahua Cove Terraces	0	0	0	0	0	0	0	0	0	0	0	0	37	34	2	0
Eckert Bayou Point	—	—	—	—	—	—	—	0	15	0	22	0	0	0	0	0
Gangs Bayou	0	0	0	0	5	3	0	0	0	0	0	0	0	0	0	1
HGNC Evia Island	—	—	—	—	—	—	—	—	—	—	—	—	—	50	0	23
Jig Saw Island	0	0	0	0	0	0	0	0	2	0	0	0	0	0	0	0
Jumbilee Cove/Live Oak Grove	—	—	—	—	—	—	8	0	0	0	0	0	0	0	12	9
Little Pelican Island	0	0	0	0	6	0	15	0	0	0	0	0	0	15	0	0
Magnolia Compress #4	40	15	0	0	0	0	0	0	0	0	0	0	0	0	0	0
Marker 52 Spoil Island	0	0	0	0	0	0	0	0	5	0	0	0	0	0	0	0
McAllis Point	0	0	0	0	40	4	0	0	0	0	0	0	0	0	0	0
Mensell Bayou Point	0	0	45	0	0	0	1	2	0	0	0	0	0	0	0	0
Moody Compress	—	—	—	—	—	—	—	—	—	26	10	15	0	7	13	0
Pelican Island	56	43	85	25	15	0	0	0	0	0	0	0	0	0	0	0
San Luis Pass	0	6	0	0	0	0	2	0	0	0	3	3	2	0	0	0
Smith Point Island	0	0	0	0	0	0	0	0	10	0	10	0	0	0	0	0
Snake Cove Point	0	0	0	0	0	0	15	0	0	0	0	0	0	0	0	0
Snake Island	0	0	0	9	0	0	0	0	0	0	0	0	0	0	0	0
Swan Lake	0	0	0	0	0	16	0	0	0	15	20	50	8	15	0	9
West Bay Mooring Facility	—	—	—	—	—	—	—	—	—	—	—	—	—	—	6	0

Table A-10. (cont'd)

Colony	1988	1989	1990	1991	1992	1993	1994	1995	1996	1997	1998	1999	2000	2001	2002	2003
Galveston Bay; Brazoria Co.																
Arcadia Reef	0	0	0	0	0	0	0	0	0	4	0	0	0	0	0	0
Bastrop Bay	0	20	0	0	0	5	0	0	5	0	0	0	0	0	10	0
Drum Bay	2	3	0	0	0	0	0	0	0	0	0	0	0	0	0	0
Freeport Dow	0	0	0	0	0	0	10	0	20	30	0	130	60	72	60	0
Mustang Bayou Island (PA 67)	0	0	0	30	35	0	1420	1400	24	10	1400	0	1200	375	1100	200
San Luis Island	0	0	0	0	0	0	0	4	0	0	0	0	0	0	0	0
Brazoria Co. Wetlands; Brazoria Co.																
Cedar Lakes	25	10	0	0	0	0	0	0	0	0	0	0	0	0	0	0
Wolf Lake Skimmer Area	—	—	—	—	—	15	0	15	23	24	46	100	0	0	65	0
Matagorda Bay; Matagorda Co.																
Dressing Point	0	0	25	0	0	0	0	0	0	2	0	0	0	0	0	0
Sundown Island	0	4	10	0	0	0	30	0	0	3	5	8	15	0	0	12
Matagorda Bay; Cahoun Co.																
Matagorda Bay Spoil 39-51	3	0	0	0	0	0	0	0	0	0	0	0	0	0	0	0
Matagorda Wtlds; Matagorda Co.																
STP Cooling Reservoir	—	—	—	—	—	—	905	0	0	0	0	0	650	744	424	184
Victoria Co. Wetlands; Victoria Co.																
Gravel Pits	—	—	—	—	—	15	0	0	0	0	0	0	0	0	0	0
Lavaca Bay; Calhoun Co.																
Lavaca Bay Spoil (51-63)	7	0	0	0	25	0	0	0	30	25	0	10	0	0	0	0
Lavaca Bay Spoil (63-77)	10	0	0	15	0	0	60	0	85	0	0	0	0	0	0	0
Mouth of Chocolate Bayou	0	10	60	67	11	0	75	0	30	90	0	2	75	8	48	35
Mouth of Lavaca River	10	0	0	20	40	0	0	0	0	0	0	0	0	40	3	0
Point Comfort Alcoa	25	0	0	0	0	0	0	0	0	0	0	0	0	0	0	0
Totals	178	111	225	166	177	61	2541	1421	249	229	1517	324	2055	1360	1834	511

Population Trends: Although the number of pairs of Gull-billed Terns breeding along the Texas coast varies among sites from year to year, the overall number of nesting birds in Texas appears to have been generally stable from 1973–2003. An analysis of decadal abundance reveals a median number of 1632 pairs during the 1970s, 1936 pairs during the 1980s, 1565 pairs during the 1990s, and 2203 pairs during the 2000s (Tables A-10 through A-12). The median number of colony sites that were occupied during each of those decades is 27, 39, 36, and 38, respectively.

Research/Monitoring: Chaney et al. (1978) studied nest success of Gull-billed Terns on dredged-material islands. Newstead and Blacklock (2005) observed kleptoparasitic behavior of Gull-billed Terns on Black Skimmers and Forster's Terns in Nueces Bay in 2004. Comprehensive waterbird colony surveys along the coast have been conducted annually by the Texas Colonial Waterbird Census Project since at least the early 1970s. Censuses of two sites at inland salt lakes in Willacy County have been conducted annually by NWR personnel since about 1995 (D. Blankinship, pers. comm.).

Conservation/Management Activities: Most colony sites are located on state or private lands, with a majority leased and managed by Audubon Texas. A few colonies occur on NWR lands or on lands owned by the National Audubon Society. Management activities at sites in the central coast area include controlling human disturbance, removal of mammalian predators, treatment of fire ants, vegetation removal, and invasive grass control. Pilot studies experimenting with substrate addition (e.g., oyster shell and dredge shell hash) have been implemented by the Coastal Bend Bays and Estuaries Program (D. J. Newstead, pers. comm.). Fencing (conventional or electric) has been used at two NWR colony sites, the Wolf Lake Skimmer Area at the Brazoria NWR and East Lake at the Lower Rio Grande Valley NWR, to prevent access of mammalian predators to nesting sites (D. S. Stolley, pers. comm.). In recent years, there have been efforts to re-flood the Bahia Grande, resulting in the creation of isolated islands that historically have been used by nesting Gull-billed Terns (D. J. Newstead, pers. comm.).

State Status: No status.

Natural Heritage Rank: S4—Apparently Secure (NatureServe Explorer 2006).

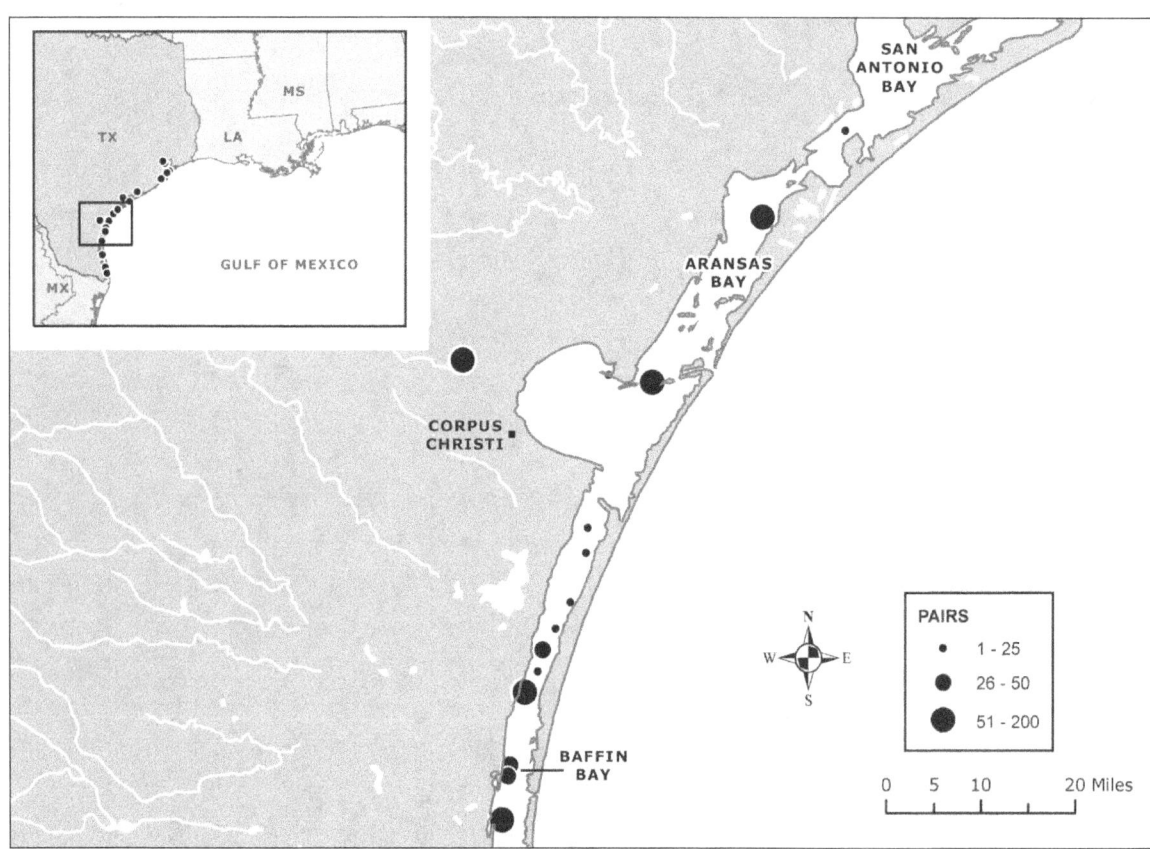

Figure A-11. Locations and sizes of Gull-billed Tern colonies in the central coast of Texas, 2003.

Table A-11. Number of breeding pairs of Gull-billed Terns at colonies along the central coast of Texas, 1988–2003 (U.S. Fish and Wildlife Service 2004). Dash (—) indicates data are insufficient to discern site availability, occupancy, or extent of survey coverage for a particular site and year.

Colony	1988	1989	1990	1991	1992	1993	1994	1995	1996	1997	1998	1999	2000	2001	2002	2003
San Antonio Bay, Calhoun Co.																
Cedar Lake Island	—	—	—	—	—	—	—	—	—	0	18	48	0	0	0	0
Seadrift Island	0	0	0	0	0	8	0	0	35	107	9	0	0	7	2	0
Steamboat Island and Spoil	34	0	0	0	0	0	0	0	0	0	0	0	0	0	0	0
Aransas Bay, Aransas Co.																
Blackjack Point Reef	0	0	0	0	0	0	0	0	0	8	0	0	15	13	0	0
Cedar Bayou	0	0	0	0	0	0	0	0	0	0	2	0	0	0	0	0
Little Bay	0	0	0	0	0	0	0	0	0	650	0	135	0	0	0	0
Long Reef-Deadman Isls.	80	13	15	0	0	0	0	0	0	0	7	0	0	0	0	60
Matagorda Spit	0	0	0	0	0	0	0	0	0	0	0	0	3	0	0	0
Second Chain of Isls.	30	138	40	0	0	2	14	0	55	41	15	0	65	42	58	15
Third Chain of Isls.	6	54	150	0	0	35	14	0	0	34	0	0	16	18	0	0
Aransas Bay, Nueces Co.																
Bay Harbor	—	—	—	—	—	—	0	0	0	0	1	0	0	0	0	0
Causeway Island Platforms	21	10	18	0	0	0	0	0	0	2	2	0	0	0	0	0
Danger Island	3	0	0	0	0	0	0	0	0	0	0	0	0	0	0	0
East Shore Spoil	0	0	0	0	2	0	0	0	0	0	16	24	0	0	25	0
GIWW Marker 53 Spoil	10	—	—	—	—	—	—	—	—	—	—	—	—	—	—	—
GIWW Marker 55-57 Spoil	3	—	—	—	—	—	—	—	—	—	—	—	—	—	—	—
West Harbor Island	0	56	0	0	0	0	0	0	0	0	0	0	0	0	0	0
Corpus Christi Bay, Nueces Co.																
CC Channel Spoil	0	0	0	0	0	0	6	0	0	0	0	0	8	8	0	0
East Nueces Bay	0	5	2	0	0	0	0	0	0	30	0	1	0	0	0	0
Ingleside Point	0	0	0	0	0	14	0	0	0	3	0	5	0	0	0	2
Oso Bay	—	—	—	—	—	—	—	—	—	—	—	—	20	—	—	—
Pelican Island Spoil	30	21	5	0	0	12	6	4	5	0	0	8	3	3	0	74
Shamrock Island	0	0	0	0	0	0	0	3	11	10	18	0	7	7	0	0
Skimmer Island	—	—	—	—	—	—	—	—	—	—	—	—	—	—	120	0
Sunset Lake	0	0	0	0	0	0	0	0	0	0	0	0	0	1	0	0
West Nueces Bay	0	20	14	0	36	3	2	22	0	14	21	31	100	78	0	190

Table A-11. (cont'd)

Colony	1988	1989	1990	1991	1992	1993	1994	1995	1996	1997	1998	1999	2000	2001	2002	2003
Upper Laguna Madre; Nueces Co.																
Causeway Islands	0	0	0	0	0	0	11	1	0	0	0	0	0	3	0	0
Kennedy Causeway Isls.	30	12	92	40	32	18	18	26	56	49	71	62	39	34	43	0
Naval Air Station Islands	0	0	1	0	8	58	46	41	4	2	30	0	35	21	20	0
Pita Island/Humble Channel	2	8	47	74	6	30	24	14	0	4	14	11	20	0	0	3
Upper Laguna Madre; Kleberg Co.																
Chaney Island	—	—	—	—	—	—	—	—	—	—	—	—	—	—	18	70
Diked Island NM 178	6	2	20	0	0	0	0	0	8	7	0	0	0	0	0	0
DM31-34 (NM65-74)	0	0	0	0	15	0	0	5	8	7	0	0	0	0	10	14
Marker 3 -38 Spoil NM 79	19	2	10	0	2	0	18	5	15	4	15	0	3	6	0	0
Marker 63-65 Spoil (NM 127-131)	3	24	8	26	104	43	21	10	30	77	21	20	0	21	14	13
Marker 69 Spoil (NM 141)	0	14	0	8	18	43	36	0	0	11	18	9	0	15	6	0
Marker 72 Spoil Island (NM 152)	42	24	12	72	2	58	28	0	8	0	0	0	0	0	13	26
Marker 77A Spoil Island (NM 155)	7	18	52	0	0	13	4	0	0	68	0	0	0	0	0	0
Marker 81 Spoil Island (NM 163)	0	12	30	0	0	0	0	0	0	4	5	0	3	0	0	8
Marker 85 A Spoil Island (NM 165)	59	8	50	0	10	30	35	0	0	97	42	24	1	41	0	0
Marker 91 Spoil Island	0	8	2	1	14	42	12	6	14	13	18	6	1	7	0	0
North Bird Island	0	0	0	0	0	0	8	0	16	0	0	0	0	7	0	0
North of Bird Island Marker 43	0	46	1	0	14	32	10	3	0	13	22	4	17	7	13	0
Side Channel Island (NM 199)	0	0	0	44	0	0	2	0	0	0	8	21	0	0	0	0
South Bird Island	38	0	30	0	0	14	1	32	0	21	0	0	0	0	0	11
South of South Bird Island	0	0	10	2	0	0	1	21	0	0	2	13	0	0	0	0
West of North Bird Island	0	0	0	0	0	8	0	0	0	0	0	0	0	0	0	0
Yellow House Spoil (NM 162)	—	—	—	—	—	—	—	—	24	0	0	0	0	0	0	0
Upper Laguna Madre; Kenedy Co.																
Marker 139-155 Spoil (19-35)	61	70	210	0	74	18	0	3	41	25	44	0	42	22	40	36
N.Yarborough Pass (NM 37-39)	0	38	6	0	34	44	0	0	0	0	14	0	17	0	0	0
S.Yarborough Pass (NM 41-47)	28	2	0	0	6	0	0	0	0	24	0	0	36	29	28	0
The Hole	0	0	0	0	6	0	0	0	0	0	0	0	0	0	0	52
Yarborough Pass	0	0	0	0	0	0	0	0	28	0	0	0	0	0	0	0
Baffin Bay; Kleberg Co.																
Marker 103-117 Spoil (NM 207-221)	0	0	0	0	16	0	3	7	13	0	34	0	0	21	2	0
South Baffin Bay Island	24	36	0	0	28	25	35	42	24	35	32	41	70	35	32	38
Totals	536	641	825	267	427	550	355	240	395	1347	499	463	521	439	444	612

Habitat Conditions: Gull-billed Terns nest on natural estuarine islands, natural shell and sand bars and spits, and dredged-material islands along the Intracoastal Waterway (Oberholser 1974). They occasionally nest on islands or isolated peninsulas in large freshwater reservoirs (Lockwood and Freeman 2004) or on levees surrounding the cooling reservoir of a nuclear power plant (P. Glass, pers. comm.). The preferred nesting habitat is sparsely vegetated or barren shell beaches of isolated islands (Texas Colonial Waterbird Society 1982). The species forages over salt and freshwater marshes, wet coastal prairies and fields, and along bay shores (Oberholser 1974, Lockwood and Freeman 2004).

Threats: Vegetation succession and island erosion are threats to nesting habitat (J. K. Wilson and P. Glass, pers. comm.). The observed increase in the numbers of nesting Laughing Gulls in Corpus Christi Bay in their immediate colonization of newly constructed nesting islands is a potential threat (D. J. Newstead, pers. comm.). Prior to 1986, annual counts of Laughing Gulls in Corpus Christi Bay ranged between 3000 and 9000 pairs (Texas Colonial Waterbird Society 1982). Since 1986, annual counts consistently exceeded 10,000 pairs, with high counts in some years ranging from 15,000 to nearly 20,000 pairs.

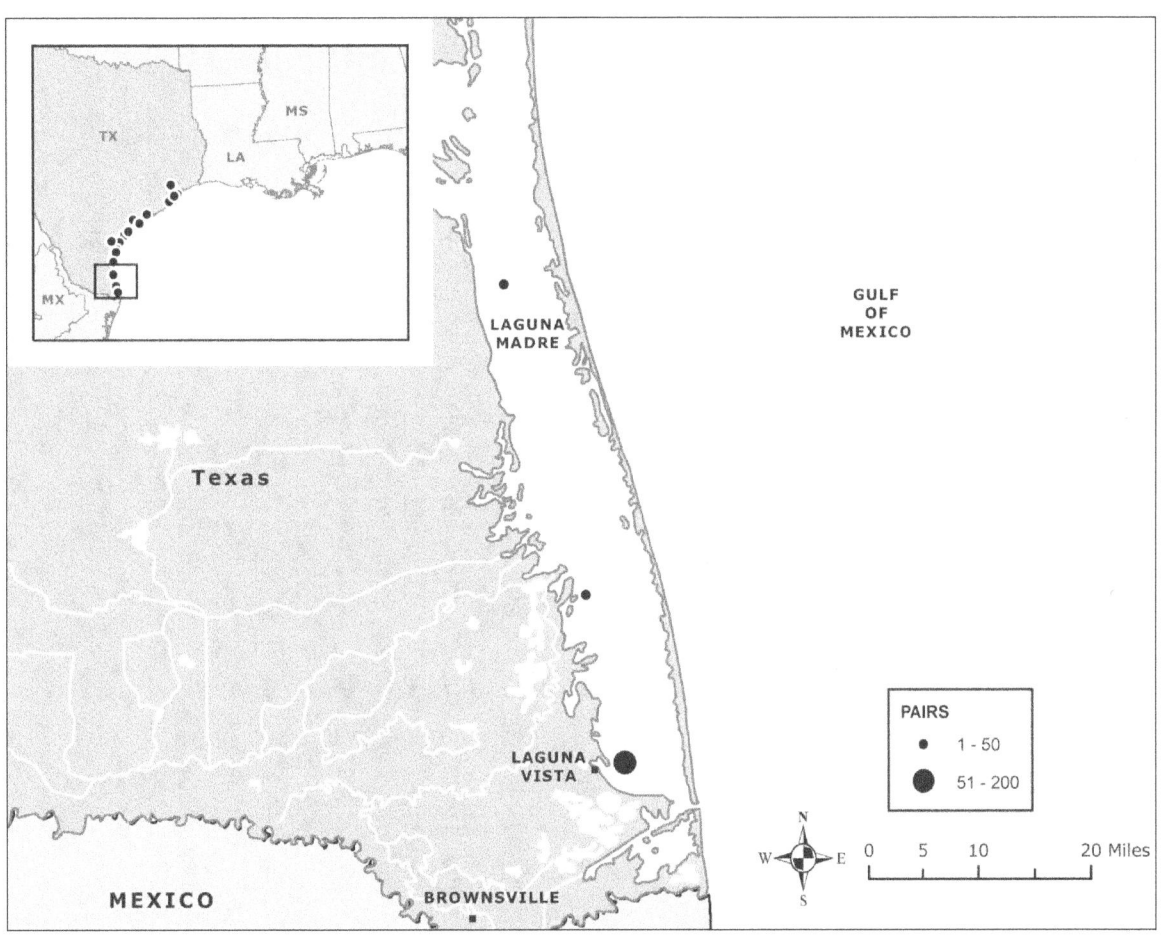

Figure A-12. Locations and sizes of Gull-billed Tern colonies in the lower coast of Texas, 2003.

Table A-12. Number of breeding pairs of Gull-billed Terns at colonies along the lower coast of Texas, 1988–2003 (U.S. Fish and Wildlife Service 2004, D. S. Stolley, pers. comm.). Dash (—) indicates data are insufficient to discern site availability, occupancy, or extent of survey coverage for a particular site and year.

Colony	1988	1989	1990	1991	1992	1993	1994	1995	1996	1997	1998	1999	2000	2001	2002	2003
Laguna Madre; Kenedy Co.																
East Flats Spoil	0	0	0	0	0	0	0	0	0	0	0	0	0	0	2	14
South Land Cut	130	85	259	185	175	22	256	99	29	0	8	0	10	17	13	0
Laguna Madre; Willacy Co.																
Green Hill Spoil Island	14	38	441	117	170	100	63	108	16	0	4	0	0	0	15	0
Green Island Spoils	81	1	83	22	3	0	0	20	15	0	166	0	47	0	61	0
Mansfield Channel Spoil	0	0	0	0	0	0	0	0	0	0	0	0	0	6	0	0
NE Mansfield Int	0	0	0	30	0	40	0	15	60	0	15	0	11	17	6	0
SW Mansfield Int	2	0	2	1	—	—	—	—	—	—	—	—	—	—	—	—
Laguna Madre; Cameron Co.																
Arroyo Colorado Spoil	0	110	472	0	210	370	76	150	20	0	69	8	23	0	3	5
Dead Pecker Hill	0	0	0	0	0	0	0	0	0	0	0	0	0	1	0	0
East Arroyo Spoil	0	0	0	0	120	0	0	0	0	0	0	0	25	0	0	0
Four Islands	0	0	0	0	0	0	10	0	10	—	—	—	—	0	—	—
Green Island	0	18	10	0	0	0	0	0	0	0	0	0	4	0	0	0
Green Island Reef NW															85	0
Laguna Vista Spoil	259	100	382	110	60	300	300	400	70	0	0	9	45	0	54	150
Port Isabel Spoil	0	1	0	0	0	0	0	0	0	0	0	0	0	0	0	0
South Three Islands	0	0	60	15	7	0	20	50	0	0	0	0	33	0	30	0
Three Island Spoil	43	45	109	0	23	110	85	50	50	0	15	42	17	0	18	0
"Salt Lakes" tracts; Willacy Co.																
La Sal Vieja	—	—	—	—	—	—	—	—	—	—	—	—	—	—	154–171	>127
East Lake	—	—	—	—	—	—	—	—	—	—	—	—	—	—	0	135–175
Totals	529	398	1818	480	768	942	810	892	270	0	277	59	215	41	441–458	331–371

Virginia

Summary: Breeding Gull-billed Terns were considered common on the Virginia coast by 1890 (Bailey 1913). Virginia was a stronghold for this species at least through the mid-1970s, but strong declines have been noted since then, possibly due to a combination of colony site flooding and mammalian predation. Despite this decline, Virginia colonies of Gull-billed Terns remain numerically important and the best-studied within the range of *G. n. aranea* and are among the better known for the species as a whole. Gull-billed Terns have nested on the Atlantic side of the lower Delmarva Peninsula in Accomack and Northampton counties from the vicinity of Chincoteague south to the islands near Cape Charles. An additional site exists on an artificial island within the Hampton Roads Bridge Tunnel complex in the urban Hampton-Norfolk area.

Population Trends: The number of Gull-billed Terns in Virginia has exhibited a strong downward trend since the 1970s. About 2000 pairs nested in Virginia in 1975–1976 and fewer than 1000 pairs nested in 1980 and 1982 (Buckley and Buckley 1984, Spendelow and Patton 1988). Gull-billed Terns continued to decline to only about 290 pairs at 16 sites in 2003 (Fig. A-13; Tables 2, A-13). The 105 breeding pairs at two colony sites reported for 1977 by Erwin (1979) and Erwin and Korschgen (1979) appears to severely underestimate the true number (Spendelow and Patton 1988) and probably reflects only part of the breeding population in that year.

Research/Monitoring: Erwin et al. (1998a and 1998b) examined colony site dynamics and diet during the breeding season. Eyler et al. (1999) examined hatching success and chick growth. O'Connell and Beck (2003) examined the impacts of gull predation on the reproductive success of Least, Gull-billed, and Common terns and Black Skimmers. Gull-billed Tern colonies are monitored annually as part of the Virginia Coastal Bird Partnership (RME).

Conservation/Management Activities: Of the 47 sites where Gull-billed Terns are known to have bred, the two (4%) occurring on NWRs and 17 (36%) occurring on lands owned by The Nature Conservancy are protected. Predator control (primarily of mammals) occurs at six of these sites: Assateague South, Assawoman Island, Fisherman Island, Middle Metomkin Island, North Metomkin Island and Parrymore Island. Protective signage and/or barriers restricting public entry to colonies currently occur at 13 sites: Assateague South, Cedar Island, Cobb Island, Fisherman Island, Hog Island, South, Middle and North Metomkin islands, Myrtle Island, Parrymore Island, Ship Shoal Island, Smith Island, and Wreck Island.

State Status: Threatened (Terwilliger and Tate 1995).

Natural Heritage Rank: S2—Imperiled (NatureServe Explorer 2006).

Habitat Conditions: In Virginia, Gull-billed Terns nest on estuarine islands composed of shell or marsh-wrack, on barrier islands composed of sand and shell with sparse vegetation, and, rarely, on man-made features such as at the Hampton Roads Bridge Tunnel (RME). They nest primarily with Common Terns and Black Skimmers.

Threats: In Virginia, flooding is a primary cause of nest failure at marsh island sites (Rounds et al. 2004). These low elevation islands are frequently subjected to complete inundation from spring high tides as well as during storm surges. Erwin et al. (2006) documented that marsh build up in Virginia has not kept pace with local sea level rises, thereby limiting the quantity of suitable breeding habitat. Predation by mammals, gulls, and Great Horned Owls are primary causes of colony failure on barrier islands (Erwin et al. 2001, O'Connell and Beck 2003). The loss of 77% of 133 eggs from 64 nests in 1990 and 1991 was attributed to Herring, Great Black-backed, or Laughing gulls (O'Connell and Beck 2003). Eyler et al. (1999) reported that predation by Great Horned Owls on large chicks was a major factor in the low reproductive success of Gull-billed Terns (0.53 chicks per nest) in 1994–1996. Dramatic changes in the distribution of raccoons and red foxes on Virginia's barrier islands between 1977 and 1998 coincided with significant declines in the number of Gull-billed Terns and other breeding larids, suggesting that mammalian predation may be a major factor in the colony site selection and success of Gull-billed Terns and other breeding birds (Erwin et al. 2001).

Table A-13. Number of breeding pairs of Gull-billed Terns at colonies in Virginia, 1975–1977, 1984, and 1993–2003 (Williams et al. 1990, R. Andrews, B. R. Truitt and B. D. Watts, pers. comm.). Comprehensive surveys conducted statewide in 1977, 1984, 1998, and 2003.

Colony	1975	1976	1977	1984	1993	1994	1995	1996	1997	1998	1999	2000	2001	2002	2003
Delmarva Peninsula; Accomack/Northampton Co.															
Assawoman Island	0	0	1	0	3	0	3	3	0	0	0	0	0	0	0
Big Easter	0	0	0	0	0	0	0	0	0	1	0	0	0	0	0
Brant Hill	0	0	0	0	15	15	13	8	0	0	0	0	0	0	0
Cedar Creek-Eckichy	0	0	0	0	0	0	0	25	86	34	58	22	8	4	0
Cedar Island	3	7	1	0	17	61	127	110	20	10	0	23	3	37	16
Chimney Pole Marsh	0	8	0	0	0	25	0	0	0	0	0	0	0	0	0
Chincoteague Chn-No.	0	0	0	0	0	10	0	10	0	0	0	0	0	0	0
Chincoteague-Willis	0	0	0	0	3	0	0	0	0	0	0	0	0	0	0
Chincoteague-Wire Narrows	0	0	0	0	5	8	0	0	0	0	14	12	46	38	32
Coards Marsh, Chincoteague	0	0	0	6	0	20	0	5	0	0	0	0	0	0	0
Cobb Island	29	32	67	10	0	0	0	12	0	0	0	0	0	0	0
Conjer-N/L. Sloop	0	0	0	0	3	0	20	26	14	0	0	20	12	0	30
Conjer-So.	0	0	0	0	3	0	15	8	3	0	6	0	2	0	20
Dawson Shoals	5	0	19	18	0	0	0	0	0	0	0	0	0	0	0
Egg Marsh, Chincoteague	0	0	0	0	0	0	0	0	22	38	29	47	27	1	13
Egging Marsh	0	0	0	0	8	0	25	8	6	0	0	23	0	0	3
Fisherman Island	0	0	7	0	0	0	0	0	0	0	0	0	0	0	0
Gap Marsh, Quinby	0	0	0	0	0	0	0	0	0	63	40	27	95	35	101
Great Channel	0	0	0	0	0	0	0	0	0	0	0	0	0	0	4
Gull Marsh	0	0	0	12	0	0	0	0	0	0	0	0	0	0	0
Hodges Narrows	0	0	0	0	5	0	0	0	0	0	2	1	0	5	2
Hog Island	81	53	107	50	0	0	3	0	0	0	0	0	0	0	0
Hummock Creek-Wach	0	0	0	0	0	50	51	15	0	1	9	0	2	7	0
L. Cobb	200	41	0	0	15	3	33	1	1	0	1	0	4	0	0
L. Easter	0	0	0	0	13	0	50	0	5	7	0	3	0	0	0
Man and Boy	0	0	0	0	0	0	0	0	0	11	0	12	37	4	5
Middle Metomkin Island	0	0	0	0	55	21	0	0	0	3	0	0	0	0	0
Middle Mouth Creek	0	0	0	4	0	0	0	0	0	0	0	0	0	0	0
Myrtle Island	197	87	31	8	0	0	3	0	0	0	0	1	0	0	0
N. Metomkin Island	0	0	0	40	10	0	0	0	0	0	0	0	0	0	0
Oyster Thoro-Channel	0	0	0	0	0	0	0	10	17	13	6	0	0	0	25
Parramore Island	11	19	3	0	0	0	0	0	0	0	0	0	0	0	0
Pelican	0	0	0	0	0	0	0	0	15	0	0	0	0	0	0
Point of Marsh	0	0	0	0	0	0	0	0	17	43	0	0	0	0	1
Queen Sd. Channel. Bridge. Chinc.	0	0	0	0	0	0	0	0	0	0	0	0	0	0	5
Running Channel	0	0	0	0	0	0	6	0	30	0	12	0	0	0	0
Ship Shoal	367	53	67	65	4	0	48	10	25	0	0	1	0	0	0
Smith Island, North	104	293	284	60	0	0	0	0	0	0	0	0	0	0	0
S. Clubhouse Point shellpile	0	0	0	0	0	0	0	0	0	0	0	6	0	0	0
S. Metomkin Island	480	707	142	140	0	0	0	0	0	0	0	0	0	0	0
SwashBay	0	0	0	0	0	0	4	12	0	0	0	0	0	0	0
Wach-CM #8	0	0	0	0	0	0	15	20	43	0	0	4	0	0	0
Wach-Black Rock Reach	0	0	0	0	0	0	0	0	0	3	0	0	0	0	4
Wreck Island N.	8	33	0	0	106	74	14	62	5	8	30	0	0	11	14
Wreck Island S.	0	0	0	0	0	0	0	0	0	5	3	25	14	52	0
Chesapeake Bay; Norfolk Co.															
Hampton Rds. Bridge Tunnel	0	0	0	0	0	0	0	0	0	61	65	35	11	11	18
Totals	1485	1333	729	413	265	287	430	345	309	301	275	262	261	205	293

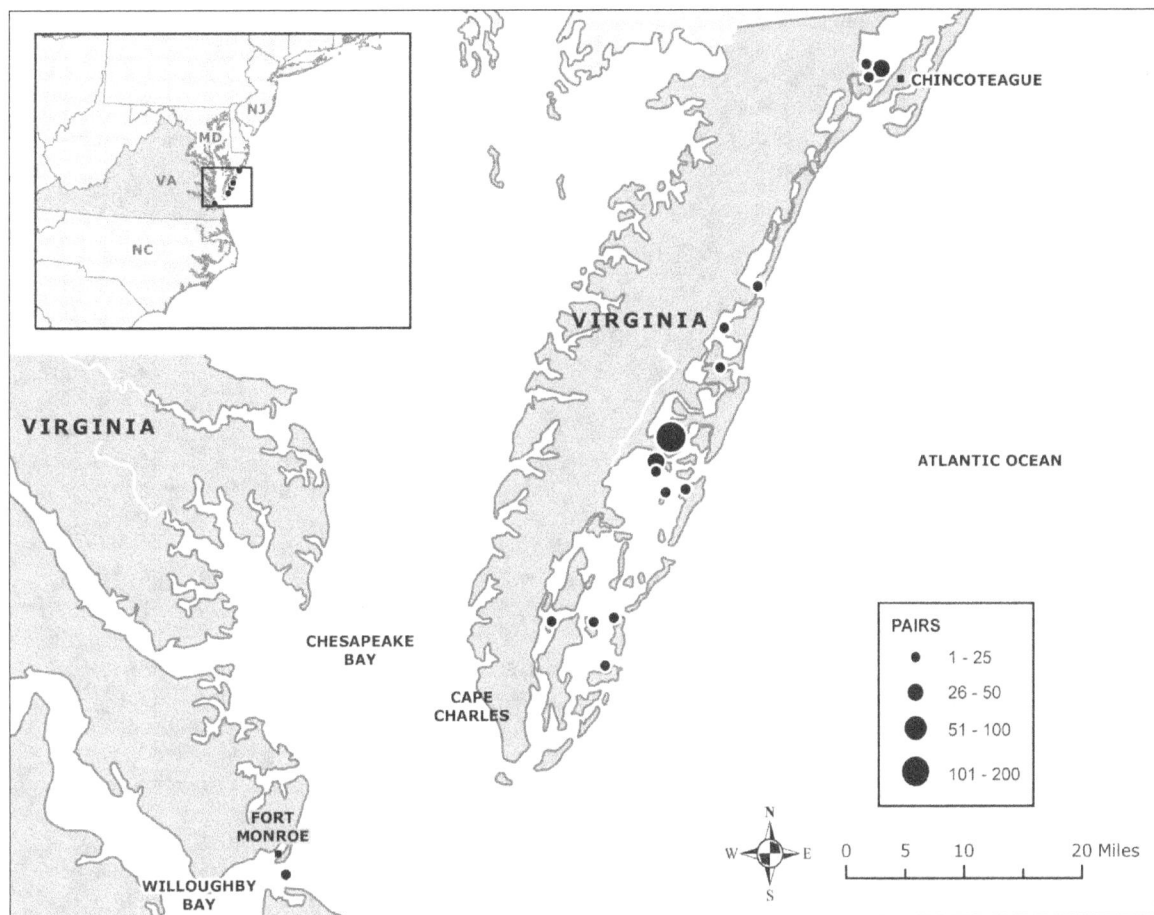

Figure A-13. Locations and sizes of Gull-billed Tern colonies in Virginia, 2003.

CARIBBEAN

Summary: Norton (1982) reported up to ten Gull-billed Terns nesting on Anegada Island in the British Virgin Islands. McGowan et al. (2006) reported at least four pairs breeding there. Chardine et al. (2000) indicated one or two pairs of Gull-billed Terns bred in the U. S Virgin Islands, but specific locations were not given. There are 11 historic specimen records of this species in the U.S. Virgin Islands; from the islands of St. Croix and St. Thomas from May through September, and an egg set from Cockroach Cay (Molina and Erwin 2006).

Gull-billed Terns are an uncommon summer visitor to the Bahamas, mainly from April through August (Raffaele et al. 1998). Sprunt (1984) noted 12 pairs on Grand Inaugua in 1967 and 1972. Chardine et al. (2000) estimated that the population in the Bahamas might be as high as 100 to 300 pairs, but there are no specific data that support this estimate. There are 15 historic specimen records of Gull-billed Terns in the Bahamas spanning the period March through August (Molina and Erwin 2006).

Chardine et al. (2000) reported Gull-billed Terns breeding in Cuba and Hispaniola in the past, but no recent data are available. There are four historic specimen records from Cuba (in June, July, and September from Camaguey, Guantanamo, and Isla de la Juventud provinces) and at least one specimen record from the Dominican Republic (from Monte Christi in August) and four records from the Ouest Department of Haiti in May and August (Molina and Erwin 2006).

Population Trends: No information is available on current population size or trend.

Research/Monitoring: No studies specific to Gull-billed Terns have been conducted in the Caribbean. No regular monitoring has been or is currently being conducted. A comprehensive survey covering 42 islands and cays in 2004 and 2005 documented a small remnant colony on Anegada Island in the British Virgin Islands in 2005 (McGowan et al. 2006).

Conservation/Management Activities: None known.

Protective Status: No status.

Natural Heritage Rank: Unranked.

Habitat Conditions: Gull-billed Terns nest on isolated salt ponds on Anegada Island in the British Virgin Islands. No other information exists on habitats occupied by Gull-billed Terns in the remainder of the Caribbean.

Threats: Specific threats to Gull-billed Terns in the Caribbean are unknown. Chardine et al. (2000) cite egg harvesting and human disturbance as the major threats to West Indian breeding larids. Sprunt (1984) and Chardine et al. (2000) suggest that protection of nesting sites, more effective enforcement of protective laws, and public education are all needed.

MEXICO

Summary: Gull-billed Tern are an uncommon to fairly common local breeder in the Laguna Madre in Tamaulipas. The only documented nesting in Tamaulipas is reported by Garza-Torres and Navarro S. (2003), but the species is found throughout the year in the Laguna Madre region (Contreras-Balderas 1993). Howell and Webb (1995) suggest that the species nests south on the Gulf of Mexico coast at least to central Veracruz, but no specific sites are mentioned. Areas of greatest promise for Gull-billed Terns nesting in Veracruz are Laguna Tamiahua on the northern coast, where a breeding colony of Black Skimmers has been documented, and possibly in Laguna Alvarado on the southern coast.

No information is available on the status of Gull-billed Terns in Tabasco or the Yucatan Peninsula (including the states of Campeche, Quintana Roo, and Yucatan). Historic records in Tabasco and Yucatan during the breeding season are rare (Molina and Erwin 2006). Howell and Webb (1995) map this species as a "winter (non-breeding)" visitor in Tabasco and along the entire coast of the Yucatan Peninsula. The species is not mentioned in coastal breeding waterbird surveys by Rangel-Salazar et al. (1993).

Population Trends: No information is available on current population size or trends.

Research/Monitoring: In 2005, a survey for Gull-billed Terns was conducted in Laguna Tamiahua and Pueblo Viejo in Veracruz resulting in no observations (EM, EP). No other research studies specific to Gull-billed Terns in eastern Mexico and no statewide or regional censuses of colonial breeding waterbirds have been conducted. Conservation organizations are reportedly in the early stages of biological inventory for the coastal regions of Veracruz (E. Peresbarbosa pers. comm.).

Conservation/Management Activities: None known.

State Status: No status in any Mexican state.

Natural Heritage Rank: Unranked.

Habitat Conditions: Habitats utilized by Gull-billed Terns are poorly known, but presumably include sparsely vegetated or barren shell beaches of isolated islands. Potential breeding habitats, in the form of sandy islands, exist in bays and estuaries on the northern and southern coasts of Veracruz. In the non-breeding season, Gull-billed Terns are presumed to utilize interior wetlands and coastal tidal zones (Howell and Webb 1995). Extensive areas of non-breeding habitat potentially occur along coastal lowlands, particularly in and around Laguna Tamiahua and Laguna Alvarado in Veracruz.

Threats: Specific threats to Gull-billed Terns are unknown. Garza-Torres and Navarro S. (2003) reported that most sites suitable for breeding larids in the Laguna Madre of Tamaulipas have been severely altered by human activities.

Literature Cited, Appendix A

Alabama Natural Heritage Program. 2008. Alabama inventory list: the rare, threatened and endangered plants and animals of Alabama. Alabama Natural Heritage Program, Auburn University, Auburn, Alabama. <www.alnhp.org/track_2008.pdf> (21 September 2009)

Bailey, H. H. 1913. The birds of Virginia. J. P. Bell, Co., Inc., Lynchburg, Virginia.

Blus, L. J., and C. J. Stafford. 1980. Breeding biology and relation of pollutants to Black Skimmers and Gull-billed Terns in South Carolina. U.S. Fish and Wildlife Service, Special Scientific Report-Wildlife No. 230, Washington, D.C.

Brinker, D. F. 1996. Gull-billed Tern. Pages 160–161 in C.S. Robbins and E. A. T. Blom, editors. Atlas of the breeding birds of Maryland and the District of Columbia. University of Pittsburgh Press, Pittsburgh, Pennsylvania.

Buckley, P. A., and F. G. Buckley. 1984. Seabirds of the North and Middle Atlantic Coast of the United States: their status and conservation. Pages 101–133 in J. Croxall, P. G. H. Evans, and R. W. Schreiber, editors. Status and conservation of the worlds' seabirds. International Council for Bird, Preservation, Technical Publication No. 2, Paston Press, Norwich, England.

Buckley, P. A., F. G. Buckley, and M. Gochfeld. 1975. Gull-billed Tern: New York State's newest breeding species. Kingbird 25:178-183.

Bull, J. 1964. Birds of the New York area. Harper and Row, New York City, New York.

Burleigh, T. D. 1945. The bird life of the Gulf Coast region of Mississippi. Mississippi Game and Fish Commission. Reprinted from Occasional Papers of the Museum of Zoology, Louisiana State University, 20:324-4901944, Baton Rouge, Louisiana.

Burleigh, T. D. 1958. Georgia birds. University of Oklahoma Press, Norman, Oklahoma.

Chaney, A. H., B. R. Chapman, K. P. Karges, D. A. Nelson, R. R. Schmidt, and L. C. Thebeau. 1978. Use of dredged material islands by colonial seabirds and wading birds in Texas. U.S. Army Engineer Waterways Experiment Station, Technical Report D-78-8, Vicksburg, Mississippi.

Chardine, J. W., R. D. Morris, J. F. Parnell, and J. Pierce. 2000. Status and conservation priorities for Laughing Gulls, Gull-billed Terns, Royal Terns, and Bridled Terns in the West Indies. Pages 65–79 in E. A. Schreiber and D. S. Lee, editors. Status and conservation of West Indian Seabirds. Society of Caribbean Ornithology, Special Publication No. 1, Ruston, Louisiana.

Clapp, R. B., and P. A. Buckley. 1984. Status and conservation of seabirds in the southeastern United States. Pages 135–155 in J. Croxall, P. G. H. Evans, and R. W. Schreiber, editors. Status and conservation of the worlds' seabirds. International Council for Bird Preservation, Technical Publication No. 2, Paston Press, Norwich, England.

Clapp, R. B., D. Morgan-Jacobs, and R. C. Banks. 1983. Marine birds of the southeastern United States and Gulf of Mexico. Part 3: Charadriiformes. FWS/OBS-83/30, U.S. Fish and Wildlife Service, Division of Biological Services, Washington, D.C.

Contreras-Balderas, A. J. 1993. Avifauna de Laguna Madre, Tamaulipas. Pages 553–558 in S. I. Salazar-Vallejo y N. E. Gonzalez, editors. Biodiversidad Marina y Costera de México. Comisión Nacional de Biodiversidad y Centro Investigaciónes de Quintana Roo, México.

Ericksen, W. J. 1926. Gull-billed Terns breeding on the coast of Georgia. Auk 43:533-534.

Erwin, R. M. 1979. Coastal waterbird colonies: Cape Elizabeth, Maine to Virginia. FWS/OBS-79/10, U.S. Fish and Wildlife Service, Division of Biological Services, Washington D.C.

Erwin, R. M., and C. E. Korschgen. 1979. Coastal waterbird colonies: Maine to Virginia, 1977. An atlas showing colony locations and species composition. FWS/OBS-79/08, U.S. Fish and Wildlife Service, Division of Biological Services, Washington, D.C.

Erwin, R. M., B. R. Truitt, and J. E. Jimenez. 2001. Ground-nesting waterbirds and mammalian carnivores in the Virginia barrier island region: running out of options. Journal of Coastal Research 17:292-296.

Erwin, R. M., T. B. Eyler, J. S. Hatfield, and S. McGary. 1998a. Diets of nestling Gull-billed Terns in coastal Virginia. Colonial Waterbirds 21:323-327.

Erwin, R. M., G. M. Sanders, D. J. Prosser, D. R. Cahoon. 2006. High tides and rising seas: potential effects on estuarine waterbirds. Studies in Avian Biology 32:214-228.

Erwin, R. M., J. D. Nichols, T. B. Eyler, D. B. Stotts, and B. R. Truitt. 1998b. Modeling colony-site dynamics: a case study of Gull-billed Terns (*Sterna nilotica*) in coastal Virginia. Auk 115:970-978.

Eyler, T. B., R. M. Erwin, D. B. Stotts, and J. S. Hatfield. 1999. Aspects of hatching success and chick survival in Gull-billed Terns in coastal Virginia. Waterbirds 22:54-59.

Florida Fish and Wildlife Conservation Commission. 2003. Florida's breeding bird atlas: A collaborative study of Florida's birdlife. Florida Fish and Wildlife Conservation Commission. <www.myfwc.com/bba> (27 February 2006).

Gandy, B. E., and W. H. Turcotte. 1970. Catalog of Mississippi bird records. Mississippi Game and Fish Commission, Jackson, Mississippi.

Garza-Torres, H. A., and A. G. Navarro S. 2003. Breeding records of the Sooty Tern in Tamaulipas and its distribution on the Gulf of Mexico. Huitzil 4:22-25.

Georgia Department of Natural Resources. 2005. A comprehensive wildlife conservation strategy for Georgia. Georgia Department of Natural Resources, Wildlife Resources Division, Social Circle, Georgia.

Hess, G. K., R. L. West, M. V. Barnhill III, and L. M. Fleming. 2000. Birds of Delaware. University of Pittsburgh Press, Pittsburgh, Pennsylvania.

Howell, A. H. 1924. Birds of Alabama. Brown Printing Co., Montgomery, Alabama.

Howell, S. N. G., and S. Webb. 1995. A guide to the birds of Mexico and northern Central America. Oxford University Press, Oxford, England.

Imhof, T. A. 1976. Alabama Birds. 2nd edition. University of Alabama Press. Tuscaloosa, Alabama.

Jackson, J. 1983. The nesting season, central southern region. American Birds 37:997.

Kale, H. W., II, G. W. Sciple, and I. R. Tomkins. 1965. The Royal Tern colony of Little Egg Island, Georgia. Bird-Banding 36:21-27.

Leberg, P. L., P. Deshotels, S. Pius, and M. Carloss. 1995. Nest sites of seabirds on dredge islands in coastal Louisiana. Proceedings from Annual Conference, Southeast Association of Fish and Wildlife Agencies 49:356-366.

Lockwood, M. W., and B. Freeman. 2004. The Texas Ornithological Society handbook of Texas birds. Texas A&M University Press, College Station, Texas.

Loftin, R.W. and S. Sutton. 1979. Ruddy Turnstones destroy Royal Tern colony. Wilson Bulletin 91:133-135.

Louisiana Department of Wildlife and Fisheries. 2008. Louisiana's rare animals of conservation concern. Louisiana Department of Wildlife and Fisheries, Louisiana Natural Heritage Program. <www.wlf.louisiana.gov/experience/naturalheritage/rareanimals/animalsofconservationconcern.cfm> (28 September 2009).

Lowery, G. H., Jr. 1974. Louisiana birds. 3rd edition. Louisiana State University Press. Baton Rouge, Louisiana.

Mallach, T. J., and P. L. Leberg. 1999. Use of dredged material substrates by nesting terns and Black Skimmers. Journal of Wildlife Management 63:137-146.

Martin, R. P., and G. D. Lester. 1990. Atlas and census of wading bird and seabird nesting colonies in Louisiana, 1990. Louisiana Department of Wildlife and Fisheries, Louisiana Natural Heritage Program, Special Publication No. 3, Baton Rouge, Louisiana.

Maryland Department of Natural Resources. 2007. Rare, threatened, and endangered animals of Maryland. Maryland Department of Natural Resources, Wildlife and Heritage Service, Natural Heritage Program. <dnrweb.dnr.state.md.us/download/rteanimals.pdf> (28 September 2009).

McGowan, A., A. C. Broderick, S. Gore, G. Hilton, N. K. Woodfield, and B. J. Godley. 2006. Breeding seabirds in the British Virgin Islands. Endangered Species Research 2:15-20.

Michot, T.C., C. W. Jeske, W. J. Vermillion, J. Mazourek, and S. Kemmerer. 2004. Atlas and census of wading bird and seabird nesting colonies in south Louisiana, 2001. Baratara Terrebonne National Estuary Program Report No. 32. Thibodaux, Louisiana.

Mississippi Department of Wildlife, Fisheries, and Parks. 2005. Appendix VIII: Mississippi's species of greatest conservation need by Ecoregion. Comprehensive Wildlife Conservation Strategy, Mississippi Department of Wildlife, Fisheries, and Parks. <www.mdwfp.com/homelinks/more/Final/Appendix%208.pdf> (28 October 2009).

Molina, K. C., and R. M. Erwin. 2006. The distribution and conservation status of the Gull-billed Tern (*Gelochelidon nilotica*) in North America. Waterbirds 29:271-295.

NatureServe Explorer. 2006. NatureServe Explorer: an online encyclopedia of life. <www.natureserve.org/explorer> (7 September 2009).

Newstead, D. J., and G. W. Blacklock. 2005. Island construction and colonization by nesting waterbirds in Nueces Bay, Texas. Abstract, Pacific Seabird Group and Waterbird Society Joint Meeting 2005, Portland, Oregon.

North Carolina Wildlife Resources Commission. 2005. North Carolina wildlife action plan. North Carolina Wildlife Resources Commission, Raleigh, North Carolina.

Norton, R. L. 1982. West Indies region, the nesting season. American Birds 36:1019-1020.

Oberholser, H. C. 1974. The bird life of Texas. University of Texas Press, Austin, Texas.

O'Connell, T. J., and R. A. Beck. 2003. Gull predation limits nesting success of terns and skimmers on the Virginia barrier islands. Journal of Field Ornithology 74:66-73.

Ogden, J.C. 1974. Florida region. American Birds 28:892-896.

Ogden, J. C. 1975. Florida region. American Birds 29:960-963.

Ogden, J. C. 1979. Florida region. American Birds 33:855-858.

Parnell, J. F., and D. A. McCrimmon, Jr. 1984. 1983 supplement to atlas of colonial waterbirds of North Carolina estuaries. UNC-SG-84-07, University of North Carolina Sea Grant, Raleigh, North Carolina.

Parnell, J. F., and R. F. Soots, Jr. 1979. Atlas of colonial waterbirds of North Carolina estuaries. UNC-SG-78-10, North Carolina State University, University of North Carolina Sea Grant, Raleigh, North Carolina.

Parnell, J. F., R. M. Erwin, and K. C. Molina. 1995. Gull-billed Tern (*Sterna nilotica*). *In* A. Poole and F. Gil, editors. The Birds of North America, No. 140. Academy of Natural Sciences, Philadelphia, Pennsylvania; American Ornithologists' Union, Washington D.C.

Pearson, T. G., C. S. Brimley, and H. H. Brimley. 1919. Birds of North Carolina. North Carolina Geological Economical Survey. Volume IV. Edwards and Broughton Printing Co., Raleigh, North Carolina.

Pemberton, J. R. 1922. A large tern colony in Texas. Condor 24:37-48.

Pius, S. M., and P. L. Leberg. 1997. Aggression and nest spacing in single and mixed species groups of seabirds. Oecologia 111:144-150.

Pius, S. M., and P. L. Leberg. 2002. Experimental assessment of the influence of Gull-billed Terns on nest site choice of Black Skimmers. Condor 104:174-177.

Portnoy, J. W. 1977. Nesting colonies of seabirds and wading birds: coastal Louisiana, Mississippi, and Alabama. FWS/OBS-7707, U.S. Fish and Wildlife Service, Division of Biological Services, Washington, D.C.

Portnoy, J. W., R. M. Erwin, and T. W. Custer. 1981. Atlas of gull and tern colonies: North Carolina to Key West, Florida (including pelicans, cormorants, and skimmers). FWS/OBS-80/05, U.S. Fish and Wildlife Service, Division of Biological Services, Washington, D.C.

Purrington, R. D. 2001. The nesting season, central southern region. North American Birds 55:443.

Purrington, R. D. 2002. The nesting season, central southern region. North American Birds 56:447.

Raffaele, H., J. Wiley, O. Garrido, A. Keith, and J. Raffaele. 1998. A guide to the birds of the West Indies. Princeton University Press, Princeton, New Jersey.

Rangel-Salazar, J. L., P. L. Enriquez-Rocha, and J. Guzman-Poo. 1993. Colonias de reproduccion de aves costeras en Sian Ka'an. Pages 833-840 *in* S. I. Salazar-Vallejo y N. E. Gonzalez, editors. Bioversidad Marina y Costera de México. Comision Nacional. Biodiversidad y Centro Investigaciones de Quintana Roo, México.

Rounds, R. A., R. M. Erwin, and J. H. Porter. 2004. Nest-site selection and hatching success of waterbirds in coastal Virginia: some results of habitat manipulation. Journal of Field Ornithology 75:317-329

Schreiber, R. W., and E. A. Schreiber. 1978. Colonial bird use and plant succession on dredged material islands in Florida. Volume I: sea and wading bird colonies. U.S. Army Engineer Waterways Experiment Station Technical Report D-78-14, Vicksburg, Mississippi.

Sibley, D. 1993. The birds of Cape May. Cape May Bird Observatory, Cape May, New Jersey.

Smith, H. T., and E. M. Alvear. 1997. Recent breeding reports of the Gull-billed Tern in Florida: status undetermined. Florida Naturalist 70:22-23.

Smith, H. T., and J. A. Gore. 1996. Gull-billed Tern. Pages 624-632 *in* J. A. Rodgers, Jr., H. W. Kale, and H. T. Smith, editors. Rare and endangered biota of Florida. Vol. V: Birds. University Press of Florida, Gainesville, Florida.

Smith, H. T., J. A. Gore, W. W. Miley, H. L. Edmiston, and J. A. Rodgers, Jr. 1993. Recent nesting of Gull-billed Terns in northwest Florida. Florida Field Naturalist 21:80-82.

Sommers, L. A., D. L. Rosenblatt, and M. J. DelPuerto. 2001. 1998–1999 Long Island colonial waterbird and Piping Plover survey. New York State Department of Environmental Conservation, Stony Brook, New York.

Sommers, L. A., R. Miller, K. Meskill, and M. Alfieri. 1994. 1992–1993 Long Island colonial waterbird and Piping Plover survey. New York State Department of Environmental Conservation, Stony Brook, New York.

South Carolina Department of Natural Resources. 2005. South Carolina comprehensive wildlife conservation strategy 2005–2010. South Carolina Department Natural Resources, Columbia, South Carolina.

Spendelow, J. A., and S. R. Patton. 1988. National atlas of coastal waterbird colonies in the contiguous United States: 1976–1982. U.S. Fish and Wildlife Service Biological Report 88(5), Washington, D.C.

Sprunt, A., IV. 1984. Seabirds of the Bahama Islands. International Council for Bird Preservation (ICBP) Technical Publication No. 2.

Sprunt, A., Jr., and E. B. Chamberlain. 1949. South Carolina bird life. University of South Carolina Press, Columbia, South Carolina.

Stevenson, H. M., and B. H. Anderson. 1994. The birdlife of Florida. University Press of Florida, Gainesville, Florida.

Terwilliger, K., and J. Tate. 1995. A guide to endangered and threatened species in Viriginia. McDonald and Woodward Publishing Company, Blacksburg, Virginia.

Texas Colonial Waterbird Society. 1982. An atlas and census of Texas waterbird colonies 1973–1980. Caesar Kleberg Wildlife Research Institute, Kingsville, Texas.

Turcotte, W. H., and D. L. Watts. 1999. Birds of Mississippi. University Press of Mississippi, Jackson, Mississippi.

U.S. Fish and Wildlife Service. 2004. Texas Coastal Program. U.S. Department of Interior, U.S. Fish and Wildlife Service. <www.fws.gov/ texascoastalprogram> (26 February 2004).

Weston, F. M. 1933. Gull-billed Tern nesting at Pensacola, Florida. Auk 50:215-216.

Williams, B., R. Beck, B. Akers, and J. W. Via. 1990. Longitudinal surveys of the beach nesting and colonial waterbirds of the Virginia barrier islands. Virginia Journal of Science 41:381-388.

Appendix B: State Summaries of *Gelochelidon nilotica vanrossemi* Status Within the Breeding Range in the U.S., Mexico, and Caribbean[a]

MEXICO

Baja California and Baja California Sur

Summary: Gull-billed Terns are found very locally in Baja California and the only significant populations are in the lower Colorado River delta region and adjacent agricultural valleys in the extreme northeastern portion of the state (Molina and Erwin 2006). Friedmann et al. (1950) cited possibly the first nesting of Gull-billed Terns at Isla Montague at the mouth of the Colorado River, based on specimens taken there on 16 May 1915. Currently, there are two known breeding colonies in Baja California; Isla Montague, where the number of nesting pairs ranged from 150 to 200 in 1992 to 30 in 2003 (Palacios and Mellink 1993, EM, EP), and Cerro Prieto Geothermal Area (Campo Geotérmico Cerro Prieto) in the Mexicali Valley, where 100 to 234 pairs nested from 1996–2004 (Molina and Garrett 2001, KCM). Although the numbers of pairs at Isla Montague and Cerro Prieto have remained fairly stable in recent years (Fig. B-1; Tables 3, B-1), nesting success at Isla Montague appears to be low in most years because of tidal flooding (Peresbarbosa and Mellink 2001, KCM) while nest success at Cerro Prieto is usually high (EM, KCM, EP). Complete colony failures were reported at Isla Montague in 2004 and 2005 as high tides flooded all early nest attempts in both years, with birds failing to renest (KCM).

Gull-billed Terns forage in tidal and agricultural habitats throughout much of the Mexicali Valley and Colorado River delta. This species is not known to occur along the Gulf of California shoreline south of San Felipe, nor is it found on the Gulf islands (away from the immediate delta). There are a few records of transients on the Pacific coast in the vicinity of Ensenada (Erickson et al. 2001).

Gull-billed Terns were unknown historically in Baja California Sur apart from two specimens purportedly taken at Cabo San Lucas in 1859 but not subsequently located (Grinnell 1928). In 1996, four pairs of Gull-billed Terns nested at the saltworks near Guerrero Negro in the extreme northwestern part of the state (Danemann and Carmona 2000), and four, 14, and 10 pairs were reported nesting there in 2002, 2003, and 2005, respectively (Fig. B-1; Tables 3, B-1; Palacios and Mellink 2007, EM, EP). Otherwise the species is known only as a rare visitor in winter in the El Centenario-Chametla area at the south end of Bahia de La Paz (Erickson et al. 2003).

Population Trends: No information on trend is available for Baja California or Baja California Sur.

[a] See Appendix C for contact information for contributors to the state summaries.

Table B-1. Number of breeding pairs of Gull-billed Terns at colonies in Baja California and Baja California Sur, México, 1992–1994, 1996–2005. Dash (—) indicates no survey was conducted; n/a = birds were present but not counted. Data from Danemann and Carmona 2000, Molina and Garrett 2001, Palacios and Mellink 1993, 2007, EM, KCM, EP.

Colony	1992	1993	1994	1996	1997	1998	1999	2000	2001	2002	2003	2004	2005
Baja California-interior													
Cerro Prieto geothermal ponds	—	—	—	136	85–100	56	—	140	191	>144	153	234	161
Baja California-Gulf of California													
Isla Montague	150–200	92	94	—	—	77	77	—	—	—	30	n/a	113
Baja California Sur													
Guerrero Negro saltworks	—	—	—	—	—	—	—	—	—	4	14	—	10
Laguna Ojo de Liebre saltworks	—	—	—	4	—	—	—	—	—	0	0	—	0

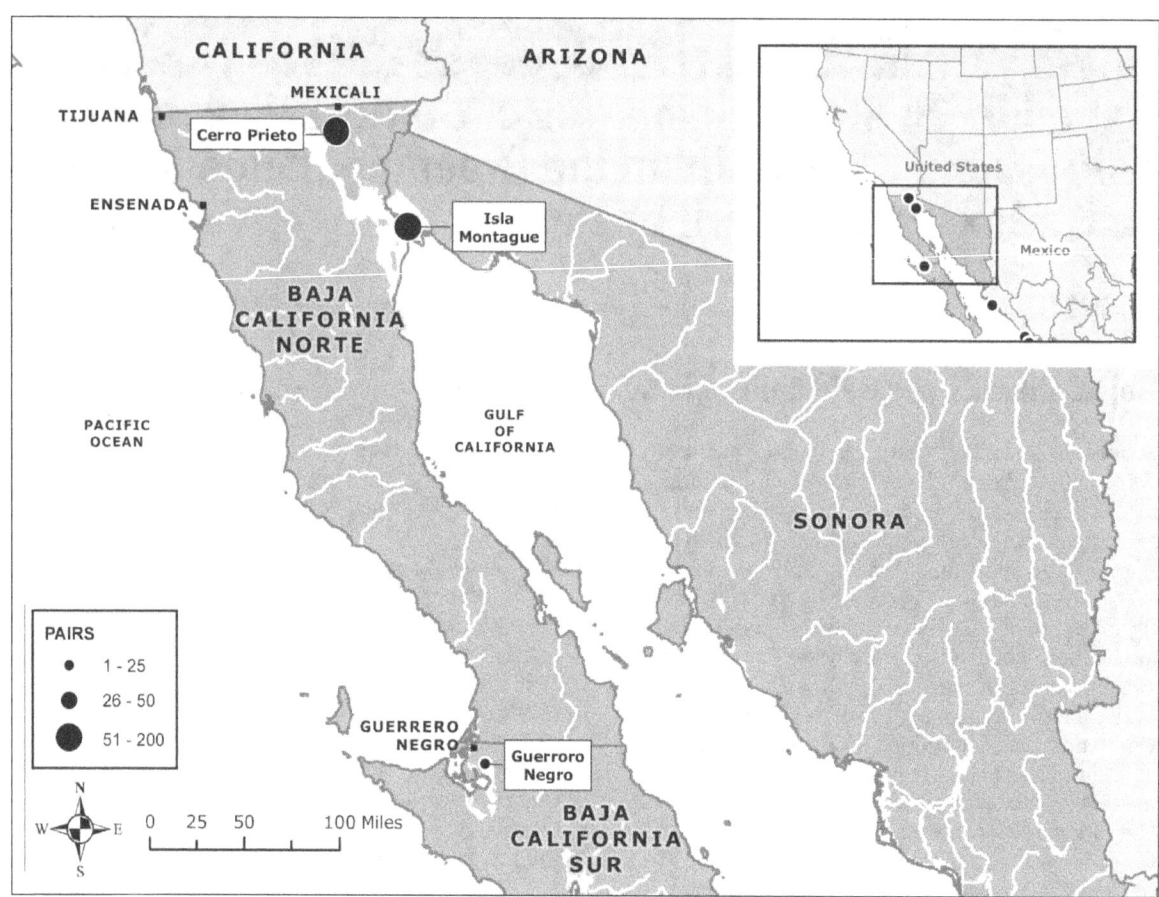

Figure B-1. Locations and sizes of Gull-billed Tern colonies in coastal northwest Mexico, 2003.

Research/Monitoring: Since the mid-1990s, censuses of breeding colonial waterbirds at both Isla Montague and Cerro Prieto have been conducted nearly annually, but have varied in methodology and intensity. Biologists from the Upper Gulf of California and Colorado River Delta Biosphere Reserve conduct seasonal monitoring of shorebirds at Cerro Prieto, Isla Montague, and surrounding areas, and opportunistically collect information on the presence and numbers of Gull-billed Terns and other colonial waterbirds. Prior to 2003, surveys for Gull-billed Terns in Baja California Sur were conducted opportunistically as part of other studies.

Conservation/Management Activities: Signage indicating the protective status of migratory birds has been posted recently at Cerro Prieto. Although Cerro Prieto occurs on federal land, administered by the Comisión Federal de Electricidad, and is located at the northern end of a conservation area encompassing the Río Hardy watershed, no active habitat management is conducted here. Isla Montague is in the Upper Gulf of California and Colorado River Delta Biosphere Reserve (a federal natural protected area), and though it is not actively managed for colonial nesting birds, access and land use changes are restricted at the site. Although the saltwork colonies in Baja California Sur are in the Viscaino Biosphere Reserve, they occur on private lands and receive no special management.

State Status: No status in either state.

Natural Heritage Rank: Unranked in both states.

Habitat Conditions: The nesting substrate at Isla Montague consists of fine sediments with sparse salt grass (*Distichlis palmeri*) and isolated mounds of broken clam shells. At Cerro Prieto, nesting occurs on earthen islets located within waste water impoundments. Foraging habitats include the extensive tidal flats of the delta as well as river channels, agricultural canals, and flooded agricultural fields. The small colonies at the Guerrero Negro saltworks occurred on sand and shell islands (Danemann and Carmona 2000, EM, EP).

Threats: Inundation and failure of nests on the tidal flats on Isla Montague occurs regularly (Peresbarbosa and Mellink 2001, KCM). A potential threat to reproduction at Isla Montague and Cerro Prieto is predation by mammals, particularly coyotes and raccoons. Large variations in the water levels of impoundments at Cerro Prieto may increase access to nesting islands by mammalian predators or may inundate nests. No threats have been reported from Baja California Sur sites.

Colima, Nayarit, Sinaloa, and Sonora

Summary: Gull-billed Terns were not mentioned in a partial survey of the birds of Colima (Schaldach 1963). A single colony was found at Laguna Cuyutlan southeast of Manzanillo in Colima in 2003 (EM, EP) and 2005 (Fig. B-2; Tables 3, B-2; Palacios and Mellink 2007).

The most thorough work on the avifauna of Nayarit (Escalante 1988) did not record Gull-billed Tern breeding, but breeders were recently confirmed (EM, EP). In 2003, two pairs of Gull-bill Terns nested at Estero Teacapan and 120-150 pairs nested at Laguna Pericos in Marismas Nacionales (Fig. B-2; Tables 3, B-2; Palacios and Mellink 2007). In 2005, only Laguna Pericos was occupied with 160 pairs. Thus Laguna Pericos, one of only three colony sites in southern west Mexico, supports the largest population away from the Colorado River delta.

In Sinaloa, Gull-billed Terns are known only from a single colony. Gonzalez-Bernal et al. (2003) first documented a small breeding colony on Isla El Rancho (approximately 120 ha) in northern Bahia Santa Maria in 2000, although a specimen in breeding condition was collected in 1934 from nearby Isla Laricion (Molina and Erwin 2006).

The colony at Isla El Rancho contained five, 23, five, and 15 pairs in 2000, 2001, 2002, and 2003, respectively (Fig. B-2; Tables 3, B-2; X. Vega, pers. comm.). In 2005, only 1-2 pairs attempted to nest (KCM).

Van Rossem (1945) presumed the Gull-billed Tern to be a common breeder near Bahia Tobari in Sonora, based on specimens he collected in the area. Breeding surveys in 1994 by Palacios and Mellink (1995) and focused surveys in 2003 and 2005 failed to document nesting colonies in all of coastal Sonora (Palacios and Mellink 2007).

This species is a common winter visitor in the larger coastal estuaries in Sinaloa and, throughout Marismas Nacionales and the San Blas area in Nayarit. Non-breeding birds also occur widely in small numbers in major estuaries, along the coast, and in adjacent agricultural zones in the Colorado River delta in Sonora (KCM). The species was mapped as a winter visitor along the coast in Colima (Howell and Webb 1995), but not found on non-breeding surveys of Laguna Cuyutlan (Mellink and de la Riva 2005).

Population Trends: No information on trends is available for any of these states. The only site that has been monitored regularly is Isla El Rancho;

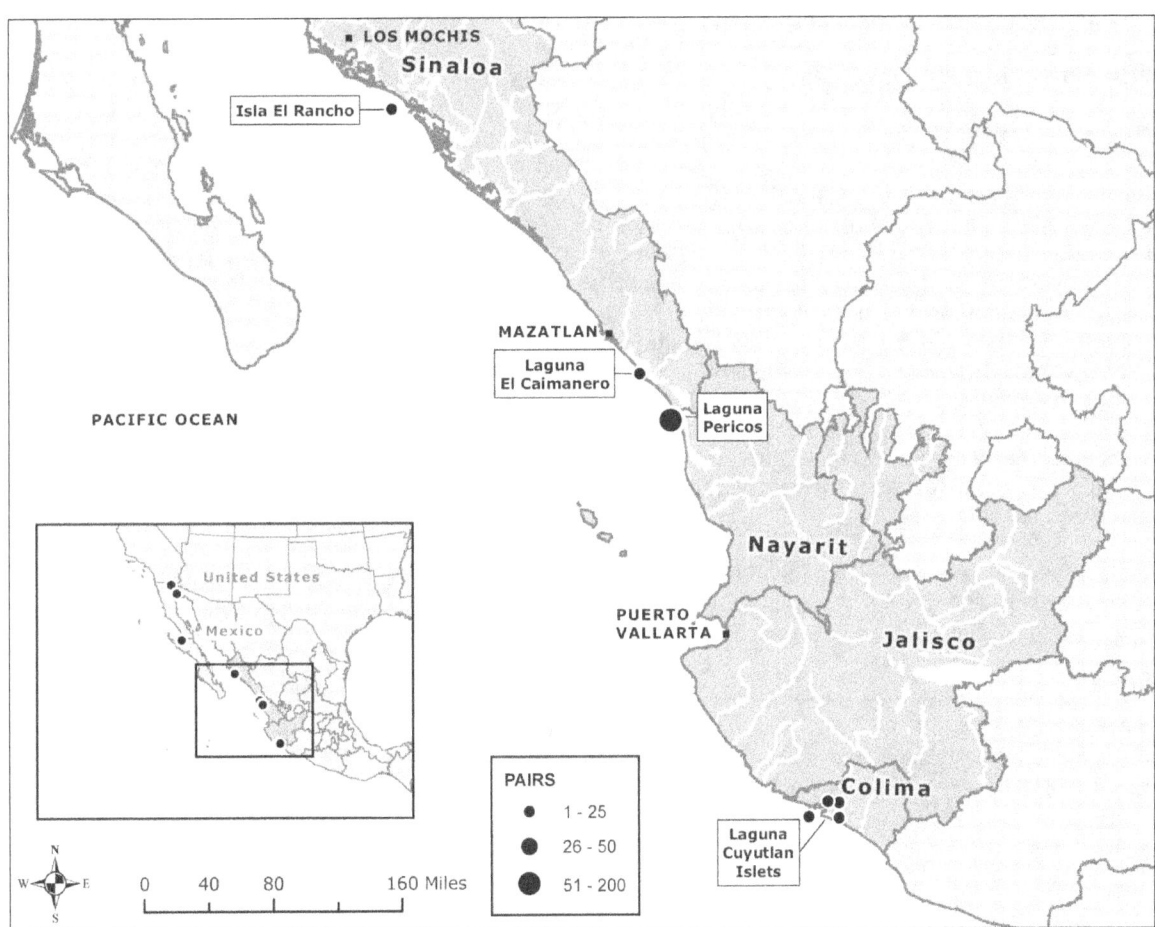

Figure B-2. Locations and sizes of Gull-billed Tern colonies in coastal southwest Mexico, 2003.

the estimated number of breeding pairs has varied from one or two to 23 pairs since the colony's discovery in 2000. If a colony did exist early in the 20th century at Bahia Tobari, Sonora it now appears that the species has become extirpated as a breeder in the state.

Research/Monitoring: Comprehensive surveys were conducted in Colima and Nayarit in 2003 and 2005. Breeding Gull-billed Terns have been surveyed annually in the Bahia Santa Maria-Ensenada Pabellones area in Sinaloa during general waterbird colony surveys since 2000. Munoz del Viejo et al. (2004) documented the reproductive success of seabirds, which included Gull-billed Terns, in Bahia Santa Maria. No surveys or research for Gull-billed Terns have been conducted in Sonora.

Conservation/Management Activities: No specific management actions directed toward nesting colonies occur in Colima, Nayarit, and Sonora. Although Isla El Rancho lies within the Gulf of California Island Park System and is included in the Conservation of Critical Coastal Ecosystems in Mexico program for Bahia Santa Maria, no specific management activities are directed toward the nesting colonies. Local educational programs work to increase awareness of the wildlife values of the bay (X. Vega, pers. comm.). Except for protective signage, no special conservation management actions have been practiced in Sinaloa.

State Status: No status for all states.

Natural Heritage Rank: Unranked for all states.

Habitat Conditions: In Colima, Gull-billed Terns nest on small islets in sandy mudflats with saltmarsh vegetation dominated by glasswort (*Salicornia sp.*) and saltwort (*Batis maritime*; Palacios and Mellink 2007). Foraging information is not available. In Nayarit, Gull-billed Terns nest on sandy barrier beaches or sandy islets with some stands of mangrove (Palacios and Mellink 2007, EM, EP). Foraging Gull-billed Terns concentrate at shrimp farm ponds (Palacios and Mellink 2007, EM, EP) and at a variety of extensive tidal and seasonally inundated flats.

In Sinaloa, nesting occurs on a sandy shoal island consisting of periodically tide-washed sand and crushed shell flats and sparse, low *Salicornia* plants (EM, EP). In Sinaloa and Sonora, Gull-billed Terns forage at commercial shrimp ponds and occur widely over extensive tidal flats, mangrove estuaries and channels, seasonally-inundated flats, and, in Sonora, along agricultural canals and irrigated fields.

Threats: Human disturbance is low at the Laguna Cuyutlan colony site as it is accessible only by canoe or kayak, however, large scale tourism development around Manzanillo could potentially threaten the ecological integrity of this site. The nesting colony on Isla El Rancho is subject to tidal inundation, and the success of Gull-billed Tern colonies there has generally been low (X. Vega, pers. comm.). Although prohibited by Mexican law, the eggs of other waterbird species on Isla El Rancho have been collected for local consumption, and the chicks of some species have been used as bait in crab traps (Gonzalez-Bernal et al. 2003, Munoz del Viejo et al. 2004). Disturbance by inappropriately timed educational tours has interrupted waterbird breeding attempts. Agricultural wastewater entering the Bahia Santa Maria system could lead to high pesticide and nutrient loads (Gonzalez-Bernal et al. 2003). The Estero Teacapan site in Nayarit receives high levels of human disturbance from fishing activities.

Gull-billed Terns concentrate at the many commercial shrimp ponds in Nayarit, where lethal means to control depredating birds may be practiced, although such measures are prohibited by Mexican law. Lethal control of Gull-billed Terns and other larids at a shrimp farm near the town of El Golfo de Santa Clara, Sonora, in the extreme northern Gulf of California, was noted on 18 November 2002 (KCM). Gull-billed Terns are relatively abundant at shrimp ponds near Mazatlan and elsewhere in Sinaloa and the control of predatory birds, including Gull-billed Terns, occurs widely in Sinaloa (Molina and Erwin 2006). Although the extent and impact of such control on this species is unstudied, it could have significant population-level ramifications.

Table B-2. Number of breeding pairs of Gull-billed Terns at colonies in western Mexico (Sinaloa through Colima), 2000–2005. Dash (—) indicates no survey was conducted. Data from Palacios and Mellink 2007, X. Vega and M. A. Gonzalez, pers. comm., EM, EP.

Colony	2000	2001	2002	2003	2004	2005
Sinaloa						
Bahia Santa María-Isla El Rancho	5	23	5	15	5	1–2
Laguna El Caimanero (Las Tres Tumbas)	—	—	—	—	—	25
Nayarit						
Estero Teacapan	—	—	—	2	—	0
Laguna Pericos	—	—	—	120–150	—	160
Colima						
Laguna Cuyutlan (various small islets)	—	—	—	15	—	55

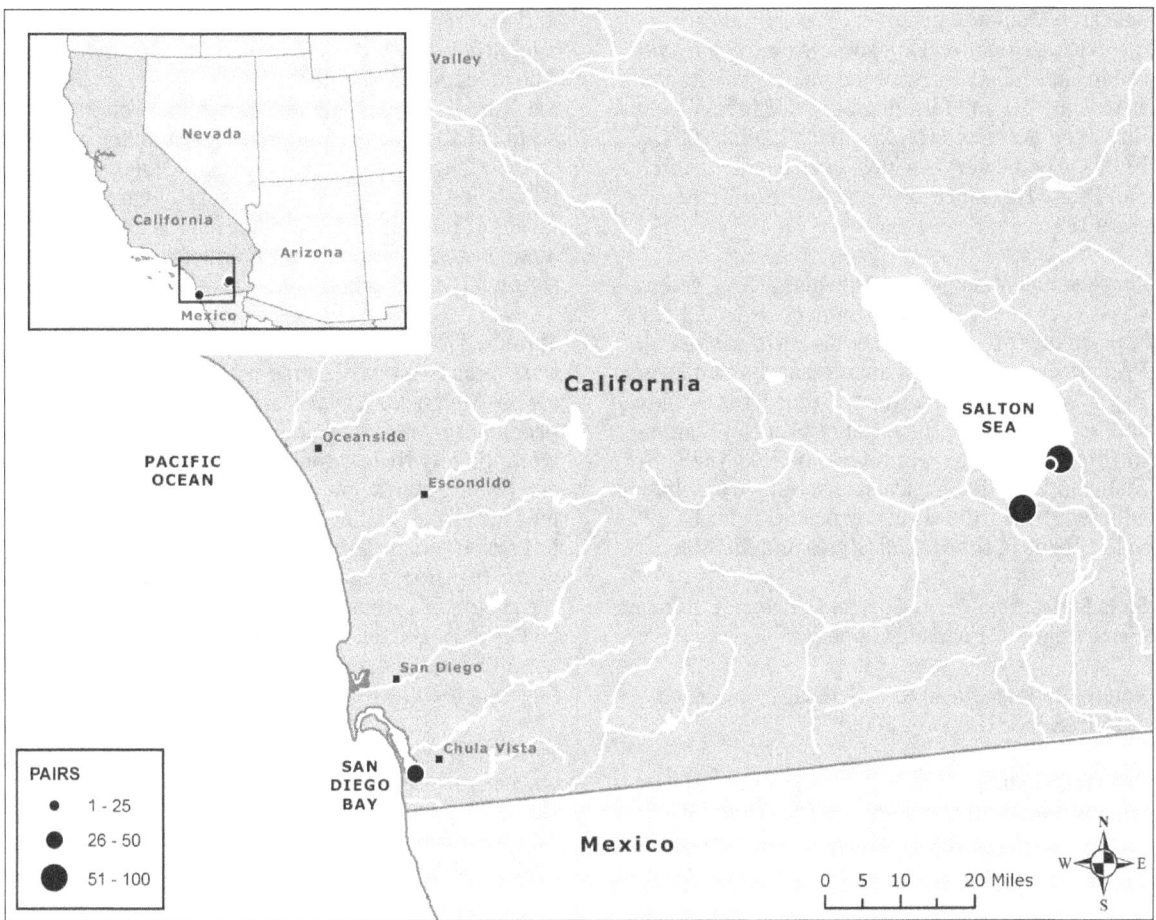

Figure B-3. Locations and sizes of Gull-billed Tern colonies in California, 2003.

UNITED STATES

California

Summary: California has the entire United States breeding population of *G. n. vanrossemi*. It is a localized breeder in two disjunct geographic areas in the extreme southern portion of the state: (1) inland in the immediate vicinity of the Salton Sea in Riverside and Imperial counties and (2) on the coast in southern San Diego Bay in San Diego County (Fig. B-3). The total breeding population in California has been fewer than 300 pairs since 2005. The Gull-billed Tern is a vagrant on the coast north of San Diego County: there are a few observation records from Bolsa Chica in Orange County (Hamilton and Willick 1996, McCaskie and Garrett 2001, 2004), the Santa Clara River in Ventura County (B. Obst, pers. comm.), the Santa Ynez River in Santa Barbara County (Lehman 1994), and Venice Beach in Los Angeles County (McCaskie and Garrett 2005). There are a few mid-winter records for the south end of the Salton Sea, but this species is generally absent from California from late September through February.

Population Trends: Pemberton (1927) first documented the presence of the Gull-billed Tern at the Salton Sea in 1927, estimating the population to be 500 pairs. As summarized by Remsen (1978), the population declined to fewer than 200 pairs by 1937, from 40 to 75 pairs through the 1950s, and to only 17 pairs in 1976. Since 1986, when 75 pairs were reported to have nested (Patten et al. 2003), Gull-billed Terns have rebounded and the population size at the Salton Sea has stabilized at 100 to 170 pairs annually during the period from 1992–2004 (Molina 2004, KCM). Nesting has occurred primarily along the southern shore in up to four sites, with occasional nesting near the northeastern shore.

Gull-billed Terns first nested at the saltworks within the South San Diego Bay unit of the San Diego Bay NWR in 1986. The population increased to 30 pairs in 1992, varied between eight and 20 pairs through the remainder of the 1990s, and steadily climbed to 52 pairs in 2006 (R. T. Patton, pers. comm.). Parnell et al. (1995) estimated the California population at less than 400 pairs, while recent surveys indicate that fewer than 300 pairs nest annually in the state (Tables 3, B-3).

Research/Monitoring: Aspects of parental care, population trends, colony success, and colony site use in Gull-billed Terns breeding at the Salton Sea, as well as diet and foraging behavior in San Diego Bay were examined (Molina 1999, Molina 2004, KCM). Annual surveys have been conducted in San Diego Bay since 1986 and at the Salton Sea since 1991.

Conservation/Management Activities: Three colony sites occur on NWR lands. Signage or fencing is in place to restrict public access at these sites. Predator control is implemented at the San Diego Bay NWR colony site. Electric fencing is employed at one of the Sonny Bono Salton Sea NWR sites to deter mammalian predators. In 2003, the U.S. Fish and Wildlife Service sponsored a workshop to address standardized survey protocols for Gull-billed Terns in the United States and Mexico.

State Status: Species of Special Concern (California Department of Fish and Game 2008).

Natural Heritage Rank: S1—Critically Imperiled (NatureServe Explorer 2006).

Habitat Conditions: Gull-billed Terns at the Salton Sea nest on natural islands, sand and barnacle bars, and earthen levees surrounded by shallow water, and on constructed islets in wildlife impoundments. They forage over mudflats along the shoreline, alkali flats with low, sparse scrub, shallow drains and marshes, and dry and irrigated agricultural fields. In San Diego Bay, Gull-billed Terns nest on a network of earthen levees of the saltworks impoundments and forage along beach dunes, estuary mudflats, and the sandy intertidal zone.

Threats: The number of suitable nesting sites at the Salton Sea has declined with recession of water levels (Molina 2004), increasing disturbance or predation by raccoons and coyotes. Nest loss due to trampling by Brown and American White pelicans can be severe in some years. Water conservation measures (e.g., fallowing, tailwater recovery, drip irrigation) under the Imperial Irrigation District's water transfer program will reduce inflows to the Salton Sea, thus contributing to lower water levels (J. A. Bartel, pers. comm.), the potential loss of nesting islands, and the degradation of foraging habitat.

In San Diego, Gull-billed Terns prey on the small chicks, and occasionally on the eggs of California Least Terns and Snowy Plovers, resulting in the removal of six Gull-billed Terns between 1993 and 1995 (T. E. Tate-Hall, pers. comm.).

Table B-3. Number of breeding pairs of Gull-billed Terns at colonies in California, 1992–2006 (Molina 2004, R. T. Patton, pers. comm., KCM).

Colony	1992	1993	1994	1995	1996	1997	1998	1999	2000	2001	2002	2003	2004	2005	2006
San Diego Co.															
San Diego NWR saltworks	30	10	12	10	n/a	8	8–10	11–20	20–27	30	32–36	32–37	40	43–48	52
Imperial/Riverside Co.															
Salton Sea	106	121	101	72	155	152	123	101	115	143	65	155	117	209	178–182
Totals	136	131	113	92	>155	162	131–133	112–121	135–142	173	97–101	187–192	157	240–259	230–234

Literature Cited, Appendix B

California Department of Fish and Game. 2008. California bird species of special concern. California Department of Fish and Game. <www.dfg.ca.gov/wildlife/nongame/ssc/birds.html> (28 September 2009).

Danemann, G. D., and R. Carmona. 2000. Breeding birds of the Guerrero Negro saltworks, Baja California Sur, Mexico. Western Birds 31:195-199.

Erickson, R. A., R. A. Hamilton, and S. N. G. Howell. 2001. New information on migrant birds in northern and central portions of the Baja California peninsula, including species new to Mexico. Monographs in Field Ornithology 3:112-170.

Erickson, R. A., R. A. Hamilton, E. Palacios, and R. Carmona. 2003. The winter season, Baja California Peninsula. North American Birds 57:260-262.

Escalante, B. P. 1988. Aves de Nayarit. Universidad Autonoma de Nayarit, Tepic, México.

Friedmann, H., L. Griscom, and Moore, R. T. 1950. Distributional checklist of the birds of Mexico. Pacific Coast Avifauna 29.

Gonzalez-Bernal, M. A., X. Vega, and E. Mellink. 2003. Nesting of Western Gulls in Bahia de Santa Maria-La Reforma, Sinaloa, Mexico. Western Birds 34:175-176.

Grinnell, J. 1928. A distributional summation of the ornithology of Lower California. University of California Publications in Zoology 32:1-300.

Hamilton, R. A., and D. R. Willick. 1996. The birds of Orange County, California: status and distribution. Sea and Sage Audubon Society, Sea and Sage Press, Irvine, California.

Howell, S. N. G., and S. Webb. 1995. A guide to the birds of Mexico and northern Central America. Oxford University Press, Oxford, England.

Lehman, P. E. 1994. The birds of Santa Barbara County, California. Vertebrate Museum, University of California, Santa Barbara, California.

McCaskie, G., and K. L. Garrett. 2001. The spring migration, southern Pacific Coast. North American Birds 55:356.

McCaskie, G., and K. L. Garrett. 2004. The nesting season, southern Pacific Coast. North American Birds 57:545.

McCaskie, G., and K. L. Garret. 2005. Southern Pacific Coast. North American Birds 59:494.

Mellink, E., and G. de la Riva. 2005. Non-breeding waterbirds at Laguna de Cuyutlán and its associated wetlands, Colima, Mexico. Journal of Field Ornithology 76:158-167.

Molina, K. C. 1999. An evaluation of parental investment hypotheses using Gull-billed Terns and Black Skimmers (Aves: Laridae) at the Salton Sea, California. Master's thesis. California State University, Northridge, California.

Molina, K. C. 2004. Breeding larids of the Salton Sea: trends in population size and colony site occupation. Studies in Avian Biology 27:92-99.

Molina, K. C., and R. M. Erwin. 2006. The distribution and conservation status of the Gull-billed Tern (*Gelochelidon nilotica*) in North America. Waterbirds 29:271-295.

Molina, K. C., and K. L. Garrett. 2001. The breeding birds of Cerro Prieto Geothermal Ponds, Mexicali Valley, Baja California. Monographs in Field Ornithology 3:23-28.

Munoz del Viejo, A., X. Vega, M. A. Gonzalez, and J. M. Sanchez. 2004. Disturbance sources, human predation, and reproductive success of seabirds in tropical coastal ecosystems of Sinaloa State, Mexico. Bird Conservation International 14:191-202.

NatureServe Explorer. 2006. NatureServe Explorer: an online encyclopedia of life. <www.natureserve.org/explorer> (7 September 2009).

Palacios, E., and E. Mellink. 1993. Additional records of breeding birds from Montague Island, northern Gulf of California. Western Birds 24:259-252.

Palacios, E., and E. Mellink. 1995. Breeding birds of Esteros Tobari and San Jose, southern Sonora. Western Birds 26:99-103.

Palacios, E., and E. Mellink. 2007. The colonies of vanRossem's Gull-billed Tern (*Gelochelidon nilotica vanrossemi*) in Mexico. Waterbirds 30:214-222.

Parnell, J. F., R. M. Erwin, and K. C. Molina. 1995. Gull-billed Tern (*Sterna nilotica*). *In* A. Poole and F. Gil, editors. The Birds of North America, No. 140. Academy of Natural Sciences, Philadelphia, Pennsylvania; American Ornithologists' Union, Washington D.C.

Patten, M. A., G. McCaskie, and P. Unitt. 2003. Birds of the Salton Sea: status, biogeography, and ecology. University of California Press, Berkeley, California.

Pemberton, J. R. 1927. The American Gull-billed Tern breeding in California. Condor 29:253-258.

Peresbarbosa, E., and E. Mellink. 2001. Nesting waterbirds of Isla Montague, northern Gulf of California, Mexico: loss of eggs due to predation and flooding, 1993–1994. Waterbirds 24:265-271.

Remsen, J. V., Jr. 1978. Bird species of special concern in California. California Department of Fish and Game, Nongame Wildlife Investigations, Wildlife Management Branch Administrative Report 78-1, Sacramento, California.

Schaldach, W. J., Jr. 1963. The avifauna of Colima and adjacent Jalisco, Mexico. Proceedings of the Western Foundation of Vertebrate Zoology 1:1-100.

van Rossem, A. J. 1945. Birds of Sonora. Louisiana State University Press, Baton Rouge, Louisiana.

Appendix C: State and Regional Contacts and Contributors

David H. Allen
North Carolina Wildlife Resources Commission
183 Paul Drive
Trenton, NC 28585
Phone: (252) 448-1546
E-mail: david.h.allen@ncwildlife.org

J. Steve Calver
U.S. Army Corps of Engineers
Savannah District (PD-EC)
100 West Oglethorpe
Savannah, GA 31401-3640
Phone: (912) 652-5797
E-mail: james.s.calver@usace.army.mil

Susan E. Cameron
North Carolina Wildlife Resources Commission
253 White Oak Bluff Road
Stella, NC 28582
Phone: (910) 325-3602
E-mail: camerons@coastalnet.com

Steven W. Cardiff
Sections of Ornithology and Mammalogy
Museum of Natural Science
119 Foster Hall
Louisiana State University
Baton Rouge, LA 70803-3216
Phone: (225) 578-9289
E-mail: scardif@lsu.edu

Roger B. Clay
Alabama Division of Wildlife and Freshwater
Fisheries
30571 Five Rivers Boulevard
Spanish Forks, AL 36527
Phone: (251) 626-5474
E-mail: rclay@dcnr.state.al.us

Brian E. Collins
U.S. Fish and Wildlife Service
San Diego National Wildlife Refuges Coastal
Refuge Complex
Chula Vista, CA 91910
Phone: (619) 691-1262
E-mail: brian_collins@fws.gov

Michelle L. Gibbons
New York State DEC, Bureau of Wildlife
SUNY @ Stony Brook
50 Circle Road
Stony Brook, NY 11790-3409
Phone: (631) 444-0306
E-mail: mlgibbon@gw.dec.state.ny.us

Mark A. Goodman
Mississippi State University
P. O. Box PF
Mississippi State, MS 39762
Phone: (662) 325-7953
E-mail: mg654460@yahoo.com

Joe A. Halbrook
4680 Barton
Beaumont, TX 77706-2730
Phone: (409) 892-3090
E-mail: joebmt@sbcglobal.net

Howard Horne
Barry A. Vittor & Associates, Inc.
8060 Cottage Hill Road
Mobile, AL 36695
Phone: (251) 633-6100
E-mail: hhorne@bvaenviro.com

Gregory D. Jackson
2220 Baneberry Drive
Birmingham, AL 35244-1403
Phone: (205) 987-2855
E-mail: g_d_jackson@bellsouth.net

C. David Jenkins, Chief
New Jersey Division of Fish and Wildlife
Endangered and Nongame Species Program
501 E. State Street
Trenton, NJ 08625-0400
Phone: (609) 292-9101
E-mail: dave.jenkins@dep.state.nj.us

Paul L. Leberg
Department of Biology
University of Louisiana
P.O. Box 42451
Lafayette, LA 70504
Phone: (337) 482-6637
E-mail: leberg@louisiana.edu

Tim Manolis
808 El Encino Way
Sacramento, CA 95864
Phone: (916) 485-9009
E-mail: Ylightfoot@aol.com

Robert W. McFarlane
McFarlane & Associates
2604 Mason St
Houston, TX 77006
Phone: (713) 524-2927
E-mail: rwmcf@swbell.net

Thomas C. Michot
U.S. Geological Survey-
National Wetlands Research Center
700 Cajundome Boulevard
Lafayette, LA 70506
Phone: (337) 266-8664
E-mail: michott@usgs.gov

Robert T. Patton
4444 La Cuenta
San Diego, CA 92124
Phone: (858) 560-0923
E-mail: rpatton@san.rr.com

Elisa Peresbarbosa
Pronatura Veracruz
Diego Rivera No. 49 Fraccionamiento Coapexpan
C.P. 91070 Xalapa,
Veracruz, México
Phone: (228) 817-9617
E-mail: humedales@pronaturaveracruz.org

Robert D. Purrington
Department of Physics
Tulane University
New Orleans, LA 70118
Phone: (504) 862-3177
E-mail: danny@tulane.edu

James A. Rodgers, Jr.
Florida Fish and Wildlife Conservation Commission
1105 SW Williston Road
Gainesville, FL 32601
Phone: (352) 955-2081 x127
E-mail: james.rodgers@myfwc.com

Martha Román
Comisión de Ecología y Desarrollo Sustentable del
Estado de Sonora
Ave. Jalisco 903, entre 9 y 10, Colonia Sonora
San Luis Río Colorado, Sonora, México 83440
Phone: (011-52) (653) 536-8131
E-mail: romanmaju@gmail.com

Christian C. Schoneman
Sonny Bono Salton Sea National Wildlife Refuge
Complex
906 W. Sinclair Road
Calipatria, CA 92233
Phone: (760) 348-5278, x227
E-mail: christian_schoneman@fws.gov

Mary P. Stevens
Mississippi Museum of Natural Science
2148 Riverside Drive
Jackson, MS 39202-1353
Phone: (601) 354-7303
E-mail: library@mmns.state.ms.us

Barry R. Truitt
The Nature Conservancy, Virginia Coast Reserve
11332 Brownsville Road
Nassawadox, VA 23413
Phone: (757) 442-3049
E-mail: btruitt@tnc.org

Vincent V. Turner
U.S. Fish and Wildlife Service
Edwin B. Forsythe National Wildlife Refuge
P.O. Box 72
800 Great Creek Road
Oceanville, NJ 08231
Phone: (609) 748-1535
E-mail: vinny_turner@fws.gov

Xicotencatl Vega Picos
Manomet Center for Conservation Sciences
ITESM, Campus Sinaloa
Blvd. Culiacan No. 3771 Pte. C. P. 80000
Culiacan, Sinaloa, Mexico
Phone: (667) 759-1616
E-mail: xicovega@manomet.org

Michael R. Wasilco
New York State Department of Environmental
Conservation
Division of Fish, Wildlife, and Marine Resources
6274 E. Avon-Lima Road
Avon, NY 14414-9519
Phone: (585) 226-5460
E-mail: mrwasilc@gw.dec.state.ny.us

Bryan D. Watts
Center for Conservation Biology
College of William and Mary
Williamsburg, VA 23187
Phone: (757) 221-2247
E-mail: bdwatt@wm.edu

Jennifer K. Wilson
U.S. Fish and Wildlife Service
Texas Mid-Coast National Wildlife Refuge Complex
2547 CR 316
Brazoria, TX 77422
Phone: (979) 964-4011 Ext. 34
E-mail: jennifer_wilson@fws.gov

Brad Winn
Georgia Department of Natural Resources
Nongame Conservation
One Conservation Way, Suite 310
Brunswick, GA 31520
Phone: (912) 262-3128
E-mail: brad_winn@dnr.state.ga.us

U.S. Department of the Interior
U.S. Fish & Wildlife Service
Route 1, Box 166
Shephardstown, WV 25443

www.fws.gov

June 2010